D1093071

The Gardens of Cornwall

The Gardens of Cornwall

Katherine Lambert   Photographs by Alex Ramsay

FRANCES LINCOLN LIMITED
PUBLISHERS

For Jeremy,
who shared with me his love and knowledge
of Cornwall and its gardens.

LANCASHIRE COUNTY LIBRARY

3011812391772 0	
ASKEWS & HOLT	02-Mar-2012
712.609423 LAM	£16.99

PAGE 1 Springtime with peacock at Trevarno.
TITLE PAGE Agapanthus grow wild among the sand dunes at Tresco.
THESE PAGES A wall of ice plants at St Michael's Mount.

Frances Lincoln Ltd
4 Torriano Mews
Torriano Avenue
London NW5 2RZ
www.franceslincoln.com

GARDENS OF CORNWALL
Copyright © Frances Lincoln 2012
Text copyright © Katherine Lambert 2012
Photographs copyright © Alex Ramsay 2012

First Frances Lincoln edition 2012

Katherine Lambert has asserted her right to be identified as the author of this book in accordance with the Copyright, Designs and Patents Act 1988 (UK).

All rights reserved. No part of this publication may be reproduced, stored in a retrieval system or transmitted, in any form, or by any means, electronic, mechanical, photocopying, recording or otherwise, without either permission in writing from the publisher or a licence permitting restricted copying. In the United Kingdom such licences Are issued by the Copyright Licensing Agency, Saffron House, 6–10 Kirby Street, London EC1N 8TS.

A catalogue record for this book is available from the British Library.

ISBN 978-0-7112-3125-2

Designed by Anne Wilson
Map by Angela Wilson

Printed and bound in China

9 8 7 6 5 4 3 2 1

Contents

Introduction

The shape of Cornwall, whether you imagine it as a headless and tailless but still-pincered lobster or a rather misshapen Italian boot, is unmistakable; but to get an immediate sense of its topography, and to feel a frisson of history, it's worth looking at one of the old maps, where the county is still divided into its original hundreds. These nine chunks of territory are clearly attached to a central spine – the high and wild moorland plateau that runs north to south. From there they stretch down to the sea that surrounds the county on three sides: the Bristol Channel in the north and the English Channel in the south. One of the lobster's claws (or the toe of the boot), the hundred named Penwith, pushes out into both.

The seventeenth-century map-maker Robert Morden took Penwith ('the left promontory') as the starting point for his labelling of the hundreds, and ended with Stratton ('the highway') on the north Devon border. The River Tamar, all 57 miles/92 kilometres of it, he showed as an uncompromising natural barrier between the two counties. Most present-day visitors, arriving by road rather than boat, are more likely to reverse the direction, heading down from Devon into Cornwall. This is the best way to think of its gardens too, for they accelerate in number and exoticism the further down towards the tip you go. With a few exceptions west of Plymouth, the famous names are bunched up in the lower half of the county, south of Bodmin Moor.

The mild and wet climate (approximately 46 inches/116 centimetres of rain a year) that results from Cornwall's unique location was described by John Norden in 1584: 'Nature hath so confined it, as that the seas saltness, sendeth warme enapurations which cherisheth the earth as with a contynuall sweete deaw, which yealdeth unto the earthes increase quick maturitye, and preventeth the bitterness of the nipping frost, which can not long continue vilent, nor the moste contynuying fall of the thickninge snowe make a daungerous deepness to remayne longe . . .'

Although temperatures vary from one mile to the next with, in Daphne Du Maurier's phrase, 'a kind of lunatic perversity', there is a universal element, which Norden also picked up on: 'the fierce and furious wyndes [that] sharply assayle the naked hills and Dales'. The 1987 storm passed Cornwall by, but the assailment of 25 and 26 January 1990 was fierce and furious indeed – Trelissick lost 128 mature trees, Tresco 90 per cent of its 130-year-old shelterbelt. Every owner and head gardener has a horror story to tell.

Norden's conclusion was that 'The greatest wante that the Country hath is woode and timber', and it is as true today that for every Cornish gardener the maintenance of sturdy protective tree barriers is an absolute priority. The astonishing size and luxuriance of plant growth in a county where 'trees are shrubs and shrubs are trees' means, however, that nature heals her wounds exceptionally fast. Resilience and resurgence are urgently needed now, for the elephant in the room, sudden oak death (*Phythophthora ramorum*), continues to rampage through the south-west, devastating the tree and rhododendron populations of Trengwainton and a host of other estates and gardens. While tree surgeons and scientists are fighting on the front line, gardeners are redefining plant palettes as they replant.

It is impossible to overstress the profound and permanent effect that Louis MacNeice's 'wolves of water/Who howl along our coast' have had on gardens both on shore and inland. From the little fishing ports of St Ives, Newquay and Padstow the nearest land mass is Newfoundland; and the coastal strip adjoining the Bristol Channel is almost bereft of country houses. But many of the historic estates – Trebah and Glendurgan, St Michael's Mount and Mount Edgcumbe – took advantage of coast and/or combe to provide for themselves carefully crafted settings looking out to the English Channel.

Other gardens used the unique microclimate to build up important collections of the camellias, rhododendrons and magnolias that rank almost as the national emblems of Cornwall. First-time visitors to these gardens tend to view their lushness and vibrancy with a mixture of delight and astonishment, and this is particularly true of the subtropical plantings that are becoming increasingly common. Those luminously plastic-pink ice plants can't possibly be real. And how can anything as gloriously vulgar as the multiple cones of *Puya chilensis*, so very thrusting and such a bilious shade of green, exist at all outside a holiday paradise, let alone be found flourishing in beds and on terraces at Tresco in the Scilly Isles? Avenues of Chusan palms, groves of bamboos and dells filled with tree ferns, eruptions of echiums, aeoniums, aloes and agaves – after a while you become almost blasé about their size, quantity and sometimes extraordinary settlement in swamps or fissures.

Species from the Far East, Australasia, South Africa and South America are visually attuned to the wild scenery of Cornwall, but they also reflect the history and personality of the inhabitants of what Norden described as 'this banished promontorie'. Its proudly independent nobility tended to keep aloof from national politics, while its frequently bloody-minded populace asserted their own independence through freelance 'tinning' and fishing, radical Methodism and smuggling.

During the days of Cornwall's prosperity, from the seventeenth to the nineteenth centuries, industrial revenues from local tin-mining and porcelain-making, commercial ventures such as market gardening and foreign income from sugar plantations poured money into properties in the south of the county. Through misfortune or mismanagement, some of the premier old families – the Arundells of Trerice and the Grenvilles of Laherne – lost their power bases and their estates, but there have been Edgcumbes at Cotehele since the mid-fourteenth century, Carews at Antony since the reign of Henry II and St Aubyns at St Michael's Mount since 1599. These veteran survivors were joined by later generations of newly monied landowners: the Foxes of Glendurgan in the 1820s, the Dorrien-Smiths of Tresco in 1834, the Williamses of Caerhays twenty years later.

The climatic serendipity that made Cornwall a repository for the great plant-hunter collections has been exploited ever since the days of Joseph Hooker at gardens like Caerhays and Tregrehan; it has also shaped many people's perception of the county as a whole. But the springtime concentration of a

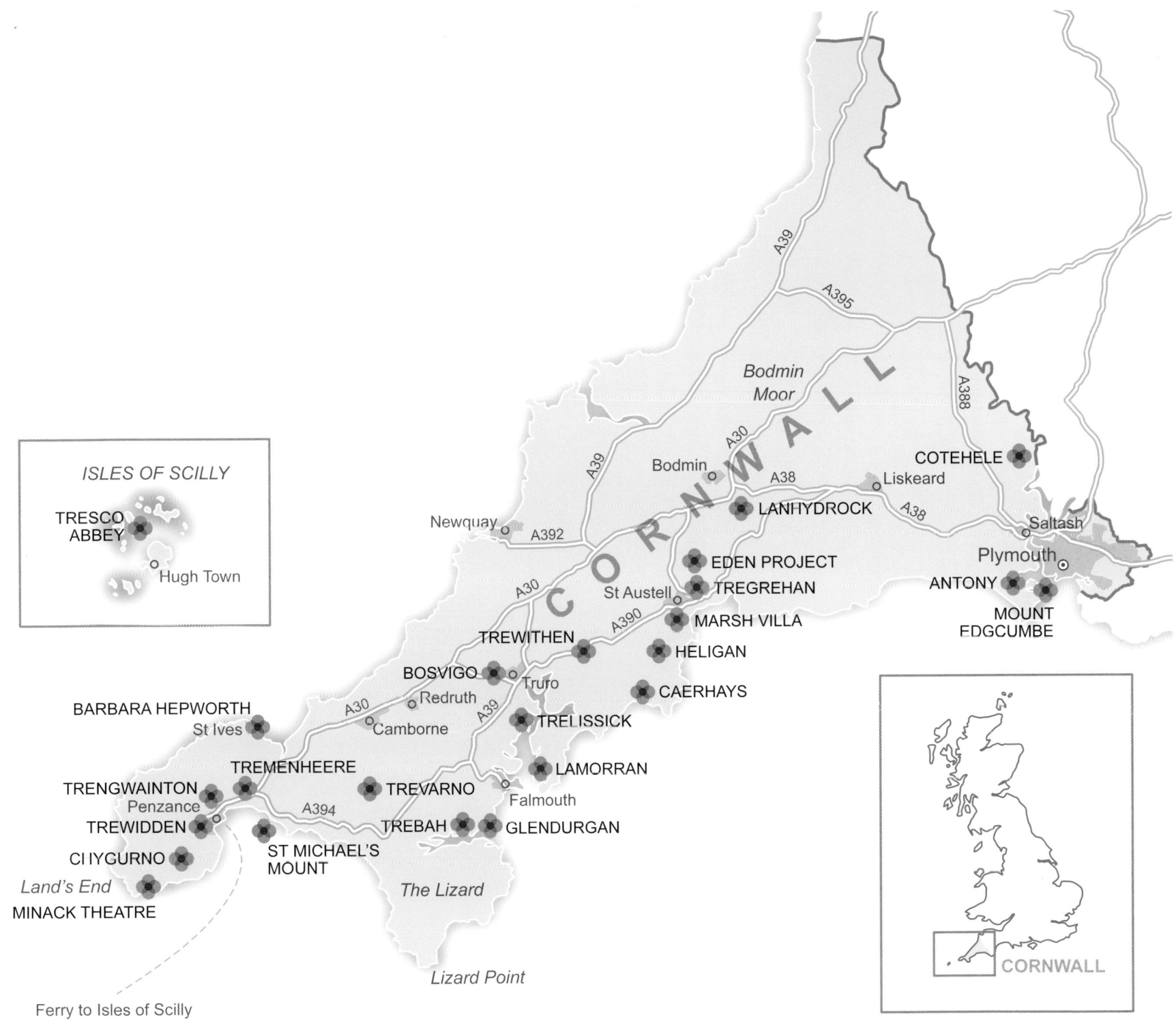

ISLES OF SCILLY

TRESCO ABBEY

Hugh Town

BARBARA HEPWORTH
St Ives

TRENGWAINTON
Penzance

TREWIDDEN

CHYGURNO

Land's End

MINACK THEATRE

Ferry to Isles of Scilly

TREMENHEERE

ST MICHAEL'S MOUNT

TREVARNO

TREBAH

GLENDURGAN

Falmouth

The Lizard

Lizard Point

BOSVIGO

Truro

Redruth

Camborne

TREWITHEN

TRELISSICK

LAMORRAN

CAERHAYS

HELIGAN

MARSH VILLA

St Austell

EDEN PROJECT

TREGREHAN

Newquay

Bodmin Moor

Bodmin

Liskeard

LANHYDROCK

Saltash

Plymouth

ANTONY

MOUNT EDGCUMBE

COTEHELE

C O R N W A L L

CORNWALL

few especially showy plant genera is just one strand in the considerable diversity of Cornish gardens. Heligan is that rarity an intact Victorian estate, while Antony and others with old roots have embraced new trends with style and exuberance. Contemporary gardens like the free-falling jungle at Lamorran House, Barbara Hepworth's impeccably designed set for her sculptures in St Ives and another, hugely ambitious sculpture garden at Tremenheere are individual statements of the highest quality. Strangest of all these open spaces is the perfect amphitheatre Tim Smit found north-east of St Austell for the Eden Project. If, however, his famous biomes were to be perched, like the eccentric and delightful Minack Theatre, high above the English Channel, they would seem even more surreal – and more attuned to Cornwall's visceral relationship with the sea.

Cotehele

Cotehele, Antony and Mount Edgcumbe, bunched together geographically and linked to the same powerful family, collectively make an excellent introduction to the houses and gardens that lie on the border of Devon and Cornwall, at the point where the natural boundary between the two, the River Tamar, disgorges itself into the English Channel.

There are certain medieval buildings, like Fountains Abbey in Yorkshire or Great Chalfield in Wiltshire, that seem to spring dramatically ready-formed from the surrounding land. Cotehele presents itself in a different way: as a piece of domestic, not theatrical, history. To reach it, you plunge down into the beautiful Tamar Valley and, wandering along a warren of narrow lanes, you begin to despair of ever getting there. Somehow, though. the twenty-first century recedes with each bend in the road, so that when the understated entrance finally puts in an appearance you're mentally at least half back in the fifteenth century.

It was around 1485 that Sir Richard Edgcumbe started to rebuild the house, piecing together the great hall and its satellite buildings. His son Piers carried on where he left off. Although their work has inevitably been altered and added to by their heirs over the following four centuries, this has been done with the utmost discretion and respect for the past, and the whole, built of the local granite and slatestone, has weathered into a romantic brown and grey lichened huddle that is irresistibly charming. In the 1730s the interior was kitted out in medieval style by the 1st Earl of Mount Edgcumbe (a member of the Society of Antiquaries and an intimate of Horace Walpole), and although much of the layout of the garden and the planting is Victorian, medieval echoes remain in the old walls, the bowling green, the orchards and above all the sense that productivity and good husbandry are central to the life of the family the garden serves. Not every garden requires a visit to the house.

LEFT The combination of grandeur and domesticity that is a distinctive feature of the gardens at Cotehele is reflected architecturally in the south range of the medieval house, built by the first Sir Richard Edgcumbe as a service block and aggrandized by his grandson with a castellated gatehouse.

RIGHT The beautifully weathered grey granite of the Retainers' Court is further softened by a bright pink rose and a burgundy-leaved cotinus.

OVERLEAF In the terraced garden on the east side of the house, narrow herbaceous borders planted for summer in shades of pink, purple and green are backed by retaining walls and divided by strips of lawn.

Cotehele demands it: to discern the intricate, intimate layout from the upper windows and to discover the garden's unusual character.

The south front, interrupted fore and aft by castellated towers, sums up the long, low semi-defensive nature of the house, and the contours of the bowling green set it off to a nicety. The garden proper is negotiated through a series of small cobbled enclosures and starts to open out only when you step through a gate in the wall into a rising triangle where specimen trees and shrubs stand in meadow grass above a collection of narcissi and scatterings of other seasonal bulbs. Another stretch of ornamental meadow extends along the rear of the house, but the most obviously designed part of the 14 acres lies at a diagonal to the south-west, reached again through a gateway in the medieval wall.

Here in the Upper Garden the enclosed space is set on three levels linked by sloping lawns rather than terraces. Invisible from the entrance, the square waterlily pond and its central island at the top come as a bit of a surprise. The island and lawns support bright-leaved trees, and broad borders that frame three of the sides are filled with repeat-planted, colour-themed perennials (not only described but also illustrated, hooray, in the laminated sheets provided for visitors). The one backing the pond tends towards the hot end of the spectrum; at right angles to it is a scheme of gold, yellow and white.

Even though it is located on the northern perimeter of the garden, this unorthodox but interesting space is effectively its fulcrum: the conduit through to the productive areas that were an essential adjunct to the estate from its medieval beginnings to its Victorian heyday. To the west of the Upper Garden lie the greenhouse and a series of nursery, culinary and picking beds arranged in rows in a narrow, slightly claustrophobic space divided by walls and yew hedges. Beyond is a delightful old orchard where fruit and walnut trees are distributed somewhat haphazardly in and around an unexplained depression in the ground. In the much larger Mother Orchard across the lane the ambitious intention is to record, preserve and propagate traditional West Country cider apples – 270 trees, 120 different varieties – together with the local pears and cherries that were other staples of the Tamar Valley market-garden industry. In its Victorian heyday some 3,000 full-time and 7,000 seasonal workers attempted to fulfil the insatiable demand for fresh fruit and flowers spawned by the advent of the railways.

BELOW LEFT A bench in the
Upper Garden sinks back into
its restful setting of pale gravel,
silvery-grey buddleja and a
freckling of ferns and annuals.
BELOW RIGHT Looking from the
house across the geranium,
rose and iris borders of the east
terraced garden.

To the east of the Upper Garden the strip running alongside
the back of the house, known as Nellson's Piece, was also
once a market garden, while strawberries and other crops were
harvested in the ornamental woodland garden that falls steeply
down the valley to the River Tamar. Situated beyond the stone-
lined tunnel-lane that bounds the formally structured but informally
planted Victorian terraced garden dropping down on the east
side of the house, this lies outside the main garden. The stream

flowing eastwards through the valley was diverted into pools, rills
and picturesque cascades in the mid-nineteenth century; they
are clothed now with a generous fringe of Candelabra primulas,
irises, skunk cabbages, ferns and gunneras.

At the same time ornamental trees and shrubs – including
conifers, a monkey puzzle, bamboos, rhododendrons,
magnolias, cornus and hydrangeas – were introduced into
the wooded valley setting. A severe blizzard was visited on

the garden in 1891 – an contemporary article in *The Garden* described how 'One extensive hillside exposed to the full force of the gale was quite stripped of all its magnificent timber.' Now (as in so many Cornish gardens) the shelterbelts and internal plantings are regularly monitored and refreshed, with the result that the garden repays many visits.

The medieval dovecote in the woodland garden (still populated by a colony of doves), Brunel's railway viaduct bang in the view and the quayside activity at the river portal below, are further reminders that Cotehele was always a functioning domestic and commercial estate. It is this juxtaposition of opposites – spaces now open and enclosed, flat and steeply sloping, productive and ornamental – that gives the garden its unique character.

BELOW The Upper Garden to the north-west, laid out on three sloping terraces, has a rectangular pond and island at its heart, framed by complex and interesting mixed and herbaceous borders developed by the National Trust over several years.

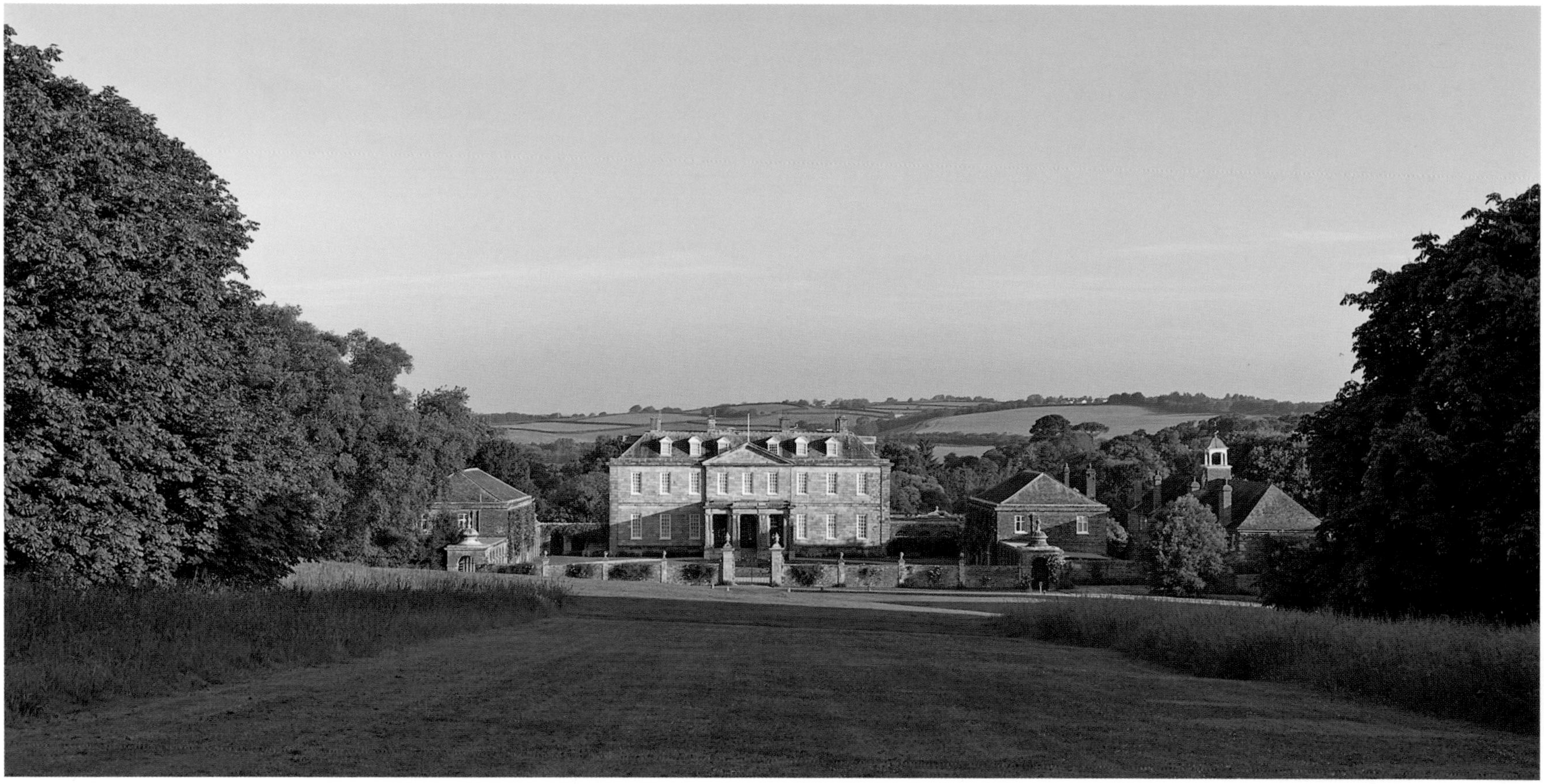

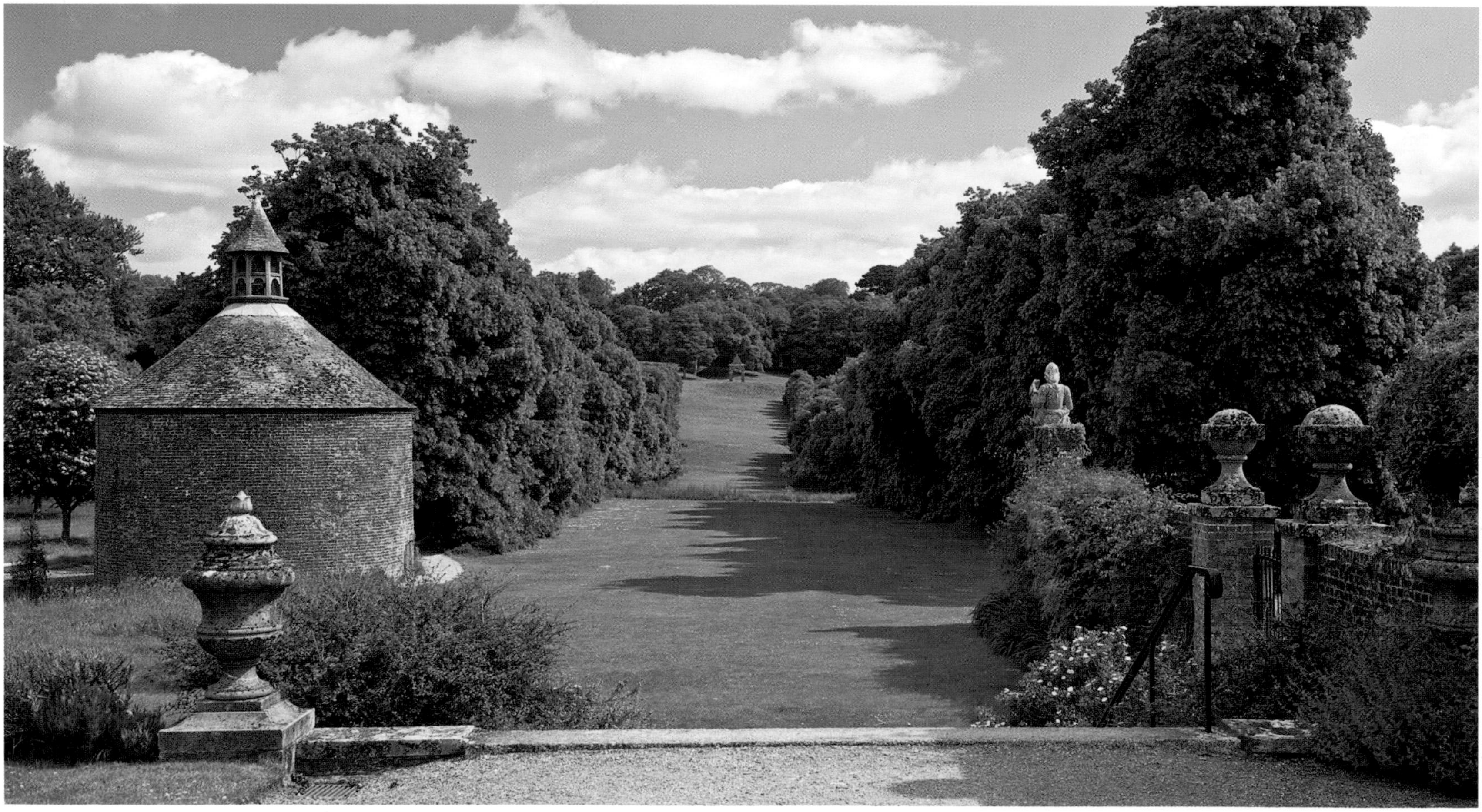

Antony

'After the removal of Court yards, and kitchen garden-walls, from the front of a house, the true substitute for the ancient magnificence destroyed, is, the more cheerful landscape of modern park scenery.' Humphry Repton might appear to have been covering his back with this sentence describing Antony in his 1792 *Red Book*, but historically his proposals marked only one phase in the garden's development over three centuries. What is undeniably true is that the present-day scenery of lawns, rides, walled enclosures and woodland retains many traces of ancient magnificence, has a delightful modern overlay, and is uniformly and unfailingly cheerful.

The 35-acre gardens surrounding the house, and the house itself, have been held by the National Trust since 1961, while the 60 wooded and wildflower-filled acres abutting the River Lynher on the northern perimeter are vested in a trust set up by the Carew Pole family. The division is clear-cut, stressed in the garden guides and on the ground, but the two very different areas are actually umbilically linked, corded together by six broad and arrow-straight rides that fan out from house to riverbank. While the trees in the surrounding woodland frequently abut the water's edge, the views of house and river at the start and termination of each ride are kept as clean and clear as a whistle, and in permanent eye contact. There may be more dramatic *pattes-d'oie* than Antony's – at West Wycombe in Buckinghamshire and Inkpen House in Berkshire, where they rise towards the horizon – but the broad and sleepy river, an estuary of the Tamar, makes a remarkable cummerbund. When carpeted with bluebells and wild garlic in late spring, the rides are breathtaking.

The family in question, known variously over the generations as Carew, Pole-Carew and Carew Pole, seem to have been decisively adaptable in their architectural and horticultural views, quick to create but prepared to destroy. (During the Civil War, they were also prepared to switch sides politically – a dangerous manoeuvre and one for which several Carews paid with their lives; however, the estate survived.) These centuries of disruption and change have resulted in a smoothing-out of extremes, an elimination of dissonances, so that the place now lives comfortably in its historic skin.

Thus in the early eighteenth century Sir William Carew replaced the house that had been described by his seventeenth-century forebear as 'the poor house of my ancestors' with a most handsome one built of beautiful silvery-grey stone.

Two centuries later, it was returned to this state when the pseudo-Dutch gabled wing erected by Major-General Sir Reginald Pole-Carew, KCB, CVO, was torn down by his son, together with a formal parterre featuring twenty-seven rose gardens and flower beds which if placed end to end would have measured a quarter of a mile. Again, while Repton was intent on obfuscating the farming side of Antony, removing fences and demolishing two functional walled gardens, he respected the lie of the land and the importance of the river when planning his garden buildings, plantations and vistas. In the gardens surrounding the house, huge eighteenth-century trees with decrepit limbs still sprawl among younger plantings: *Juglans nigra* and a group of *Quercus ilex* are among those

OPPOSITE ABOVE The handsome, quintessentially English country house, its other three sides closed off by brick-arched cloisters and a fine wrought-iron screen, sits serenely in its park and pleasure grounds.
OPPOSITE BELOW Looking down from the terrace behind the house, the sightline cuts past the seventeenth-century circular brick dovecote down a tree-lined ride, arrowing in on a recent folly by the architect Ptolemy Dean.
LEFT Square brick loggias with jaunty lead roofs terminate the two cloisters flanking the house; one, on the garden side, is softened by a 'Paul's Himalayan Musk' rose.

RIGHT The cork oak (*Quercus suber*) on the eponymous lawn adjoining the house and its courtyard is rated one of the best in the country.

RIGHT The knot within the walled Summer Garden, planted with low double hedges of box and wall germander, is overlooked by a stepped white chestnut seat.

dominating the main lawn, while *Quercus suber* holds court on the shrub-bordered lawn adjacent to the Yew Walk.

The visiting public is excluded from the walled garden built at some little distance west of the house during Repton's time by a Milanese architect named Placido Columbani, but not from the subsidiary walled garden adjoining, where the entrance is overhung by a champion *Ginkgo biloba* that shelters a trio of exceedingly pretty summer gardens created in 1984 by Lady Mary Carew Pole. The first is given over to tree peonies and clematis, underplanted with camassias, anemones, Madonna lilies and *Galtonia candicans*; then, through a screen of pleached limes, a delicate spring planting of tulips, osteospermums, hebes, pale heucheras and soft pink *Deutzia* x *kalmiiflora* gives way in summer to penstemons, geraniums, tree poppies, irises and roses. The beds here are outlined by wall germander

(*Teucrium* x *lucidrys*) and there is germander too, neatly clipped and intertwined with box, in a charmingly simple knot garden unfussed by frills or furbelows.

Outside these dovetailed flower gardens, a screen of *Pyrus communis* is trained against one of the old red brick walls, effectively making one half of an avenue with the line of *Magnolia denudata* planted across the pathway; the effect is repeated on another, west-facing wall with *Ceanothus arboreus* 'Trewithen Blue' and *C.* 'Ray Hartman' and a free-standing line of that Cornish stalwart *Cornus capitata*.

The imprint of the present generation is evident elsewhere in the open spaces near the house. The Garden Field beyond the walled gardens is just that – a masterly way of linking the garden to the wider landscape of woodland and water. Framed by wild cherries – *Prunus avium* and *P.a.* 'Plena' – autumn-foliage trees

BELOW LEFT James Horrobin's ornate and airy steel gate into the Summer Garden, decorated with stylized magnolias, looks across to the shallow topiary bays of the Yew Walk.
BELOW RIGHT The white bracts of the Japanese dogwood, *Cornus kousa*, are a memorable sight in June.

and shrubs stand attractively adrift in long grass coloured by spring- and summer-flowering bulbs, including drifts of daffodils and a ravishing selection of tulips.

On the east side of the house are terraces planted with roses and other aromatics, and borders flower-filled with a selection of perennials and shrubs that includes hemerocallis and *Camellia japonica* (National Collections of both are held here). Key, however, to the marriage of garden and woodland that is such a feature of the place is the generous endowment of big, open lawned spaces framed by mature (and sometimes ancient) trees and shrubs.

At Antony, you find new saluting old. To one side of the terrace overlooking the main lawn, the topiary cones topping a mammoth and tightly clipped yew *allée* are echoed at ground level by the carapace of William Pye's 1996 pyramidal sculpture, watered by a constant stream. From the terrace, look beyond the substantial round brick dovecote built in the early eighteenth century, and there on the skyline is Ptolemy Dean's light-hearted take on the triumphal arch.

The Major-General extended and multiplied the vistas from the main lawn, which had been landscaped on Repton's

recommendation, and introduced hardy hybrid rhododendrons and camellias in the interstices, but the wonderful woodland garden that makes up just under half of the present gardened estate owes most to his son, John Pole-Carew (later knighted as Sir John Carew Pole). During the 1930s, although continuing to make good use of his relatives at nearby Cotehele and Mount Edgcumbe and of local horticulturists including the great J.C. Williams at Caerhays, he spread his plant-collector's net beyond Cornwall by striking up a productive friendship with Lionel de Rothschild of Exbury in Hampshire. When Sir John expressed his fascination with the rhododendron species being hybridized there, Lionel de Rothschild had two coal trucks full of plants delivered to Plymouth by train.

Sir John's Woodland Garden stretches in a semi-circle from the house. Camellias, rhododendrons, azaleas, magnolias and hydrangeas make a great deal of the running under the canopy of native trees, but myrtles and acers, viburnums and embothriums, crinodendrons and hypericums exert a considerable ornamental impact too. Bounded by the constant presence of the River Lynher, the scene and atmosphere change minute by minute

along the further perimeter walk and around the stream and ponds hidden within the Wilderness. And although the long rides constantly draw the attention back to the house, clearings filled with rhododendrons and camellias and drifts of wild flowers, paths fringed by wild garlic and pink campion, seats poised to capture key views, and modern sculptures of style and substance are invitations to linger.

In 1577 Sir Richard Carew had great plans for the 'fishful pond' he was making to the north-east of the present house, including an elaborate banqueting house on a square central island. Near by rises Jupiter Hill, a fabulous natural viewing platform topped by a standing stone erected by the present Sir Richard in memory of his parents. Since he is a former president of the RHS whose horticultural enthusiasms have continued Antony's centuries-long tradition of revival and renewal, the engraved quote from Omar Khayyám seems wholly appropriate: 'And still a garden by the water blows.'

OPPOSITE ABOVE The sombre crenellations of the Yew Walk fence in a giant topiary yew cone and a line of *Magnolia grandiflora* 'Exmouth'.
OPPOSITE BELOW The interior of the cone has been scooped out to create a summerhouse.
ABOVE In the Garden Field, *Cornus controversa* 'Variegata' extends its horizontal branches above meadow grass that shimmers in spring with a variety of bulbs.

Mount Edgcumbe

The Edgcumbes of Cotehele and Mount Edgcumbe are one of the oldest of Cornwall's great families, and the history of the two houses marches together, while their estates are positioned at the beginning and end of the River Tamar's final spillage into the English Channel. The Mount Edgcumbe estate, formerly a deer park, occupied the whole of the sizeable peninsula separating St John's Lake and Plymouth Sound, and the house was built after 1547, when Sir Richard Edgcumbe decided that the main family seat would be sited to better advantage on high ground immediately opposite the important naval port of Plymouth.

It's fitting that the Edgcumbe jointly responsible for transforming the park and gardens should be a naval man. In 1761 George, younger son of Richard, 1st Baron Edgcumbe, inherited the title and estate when his brother died untimely. He resigned his commission but continued his climb up the ladder, becoming Commander in Chief of Plymouth, Admiral of the Fleet and Vice-Admiral of Cornwall – responsible for a distinguished spectrum of activities for which in 1789 he was rewarded with the newly created earldom of Mount Edgcumbe. Meantime he was embellishing the park and the gardens already famously laid out by his father in a grandiosely formal style with blocks of woodland, grassy rides, canals and classical garden buildings. Between them the 1st Baron and the 1st Earl were responsible for planting and laying out a park and pleasure grounds that, although now municipally owned, retain a good deal of their eighteenth- and nineteenth-century grandeur and character.

The interlinked ornamental gardens laid out to astonish the 1st Earl's visitors lie alongside a chestnut and beech avenue (planted by his grandfather in the late seventeenth century) as it starts its steep rise from the entrance lodge to the square

LEFT ABOVE Cocooned in trees, Mount Edgcumbe and its pleasure grounds occupy the tip of a wooded peninsula looking out to Plymouth and its Sound.

LEFT BELOW The castellated house, approached from the sea, stands at the head of a grand avenue flanked by beech and chestnut trees planted in the late seventeenth century.

RIGHT The East Lawn Terrace – a formal flower garden, geometrically laid out, furnished with urns and statues and repeat-planted with shrubs and perennials – lies hard up against the house within the Earl's Garden. Beyond and behind, the land rises, marked by paths winding among a collection of rare trees.

RIGHT A flight of steps flanked by golden heathers and topped by garlanded urns leads up to the East Lawn. Thalictrum, lavender and repeat-mounds of *Berberis thunbergii* f. *atropurpurea* 'Rose Glow' surround the central roundel, overlooked by *Cornus capitata*.

RIGHT Mount Edgcumbe's pleasure gardens lie concealed behind the trees of the main avenue. At the southern end is a nineteenth-century rose garden, with box-lined beds planted now with modern scented varieties: pale apricot *Rosa* 'Buff Beauty' in the foreground, deep pink 'Impératrice Joséphine' behind.

LEFT Among the nineteenth-century casts in the Earl's Garden two Roman goddesses confront one another: wise Minerva with her staff and coiled snake, and chaste Diana with her quiver of arrows and leaping deer.

BELOW LEFT A rare and fascinating late-eighteenth-century seat encrusted with shells, fossils and minerals at the top of the Earl's Garden (top). The busy junction of steps, ornaments and terraced beds beyond the east lawn gives way to sloping lawns studded with majestic trees and characterful garden houses (bottom).

BELOW RIGHT The Ionic-columned portico of Milton's Temple stands near the barn pool, framed by native trees.

castellated house built of red sandstone. First port of call for most visitors is the formal Italian Garden with its grass plats, central mermaid fountain and geometric layout of lawn and gravel embellished by coiled topiary pyramids, Chusan palms, and bay trees and acers in pots. It is slightly unfortunate that from here can been seen the only alien eyesore obstructing the view over to Plymouth: three seriously ugly tower blocks, white with primary-coloured Legoland detailing. Mercifully, the fine wisteria-hung orangery designed by Thomas Pitt (Lord Camelford) in 1786 acts as a partial screen.

A double flight of steps ornamented with statues leads up to the remainder of the formal gardens, which were created in two waves: by the 1st and 2nd Earls between 1770 and 1820, and by the Cornwall and Plymouth Councils after 1989. Old and new, closely juxtaposed, were always intended as a light-hearted Arcadian perambulation, but where in one of the historic gardens of the Cotswolds or the Home Counties – Sudeley Castle or

Painshill, for example – the different parts would have been kept crisply demarcated, here their lines have been harmoniously blurred by the luxuriance of Cornwall's plant growth.

Working clockwise from the head of the staircase in the Italian Garden, the complex of garden spaces jumps about both nationally and chronologically. In turn you discover the New Zealand Garden, complete with geyser (1989); the sophisticated French Garden (1803) with a conservatory, a clipped parterre and a pool; a fern dell (1789); the graciously lawned and tree-shaded English Garden (c.1770) with an eccentric little temple that has a prominent Doric portico above slanting doors and windows; and an American shrub garden (1989). The semicircular parterre at the top of the slope, first laid out as a rose garden in the nineteenth century, has been replanted with modern scented roses including 'Impératrice Joséphine', 'Beauty of Rosemawr', 'Cardinal de Richelieu' and 'Gloire Lyonnaise'; and there are two other modern gardens at the heart of the complex: the

Jubilee Garden, a long narrow enclosure formalized by standard hornbeams and pyramidal yews, and the New Relic Garden, also architectural in nature, with a strong-boned pergola, square beds and a substantial urn. Paths wind throughout, escaping through a venerable old ilex hedge – externally somewhat battered, internally airily bald – through to the batteries built in 1747 and 1863 to overlook the city and Plymouth Sound.

Mount Edgcumbe has another formal layout: the Earl's Garden next to the house (now a museum, and having lost its central cupola, looking as if it too had strayed in from Legoland). On the east side a lawn studded with geometric flower beds, urns and statues is overlooked by an early-nineteenth-century summer house, and there are other garden buildings along the curving pattern of paths, notably a marvellously elaborate late-eighteenth-century shell seat. The land, terraced behind the house, rises quite steeply to the perimeter, where fine 100-year-old shelterbelt trees – *Quercus ilex* and pairs of pines and chestnuts – were planted as shelter for the even older cedars of Lebanon and other rare trees within the garden.

Above the Earl's Garden is a new departure: a National Collection of some 1,000 camellia cultivars, built around those brought back from the wild by George Forrest and those bred by J.C. Williams of Caerhays. Divided largely by nationality, they are thickly planted in long grass alongside paths beneath the shelter of native trees and woven around a natural amphitheatre and Milton's Temple. Beyond the circular camellia walk, there's a fine view of the park. If you haven't the time to walk in this, at least drive through it, past the Maker Church to Fort Picklecombe through woods that in spring are a haze of bluebells, and take a final view back across Mount Edgcumbe's magnificent peninsula. Although it has lost its privileged privacy, it must rank as one of Britain's finest country parks.

BELOW LEFT Purple-leaved *Pittosporum tenuifolium* 'Tom Thumb' and white-flowered libertias filling the foreground of the New Zealand Garden. Both the 7th and the 8th Earls of Mount Edgcumbe were born in New Zealand.

BELOW RIGHT A gravel path winds between phormiums and grey-mounded *Brachyglottis* 'Sunshine', curving past a pittosporum hedge towards a focally placed *Cordyline australis*, all coming together in a tapestry of green and grey.

The Eden Project

Eden may have been the original garden, but the Project is of course not a garden at all, at least in the accepted meaning of the word; indeed Tim Smit introduces it variously as 'a marvellous piece of science-related architecture', a 'living theatre' and a 'place in the heart'. It therefore really has no business featuring in this book, but it's such an extraordinary horticultural – and architectural – experience, and now so indelibly part of the Cornish landscape, that the word may legitimately be stretched to the limits of its considerable elasticity.

The story of the creation of Eden is by now almost as well known as that of the Creation itself, and it must surely be one of the few British attractions that is regularly mentioned in traffic reports during high days and holidays as a motorists' black spot. It started in 1999 and took three years, opening to the public in March 2001. Nicholas Grimshaw's giant sliced golf balls, likened in a 2003 'yours disgusted of Tunbridge Wells' *Country Life* article to bubbles of washing-up liquid in a dirty sink, were for some considerable time the bald and naked cynosure of a scheme lauded (though not by *Country Life*, obviously) as the eighth wonder of the world. Now, eleven years on, they are anchored in their inverted china clay bowl as much by the vegetation outside as by the plant life inhabiting – and in one case at least threatening to burst out of – their host biomes.

The place to start is these wonderful structures – the elephants in the elephant trap. The Rainforest Biome is the more alien and exhilarating of the two, host to over 2,000 rampantly exotic plants from the humid tropics. It's not imperative to puff right the way up to the top of the wobbly metal staircase: the view at the halfway point, where the jungle giants are at close range but still matched for drama by the great expanse of sky and clouds visible through the inflated ethylene tetrafluoroethylene (ETFE) glass 'pillows', is just as rewarding and considerably less exhausting. The warm temperate Mediterranean Biome focuses on plants from the Mediterranean, South Africa and California – holiday destinations, in other words – and there is more of a feeling of a Chelsea show garden about some of the exhibits there.

But for many gardeners, the way the biomes have been grounded into their rocky amphitheatre is probably the most interesting and rewarding part of the place. The rim of the bowl is composed of trees and slabs of exposed rock face; further down, the external landscape follows the overall Eden philosophy of setting plants in their climatic and geographical context: Cornish wild flowers segue into Atlantic woodland, and

so on. Visually the effect is two-tier: the plantings at the top are congregated in blocks, giving an attractive terraced effect, while the plantings around the biomes are smaller in scale and more fragmented. There is much to read and learn, but also groups of plants to pass admiringly by, and strange wild figures to catch the eye – something, indeed, for all the family.

One of my grandparents' strange household objects was an early electric table lamp in the shape of an Amazonian warrior; the attached plaque named her the 'Spirit of Electricity' (judging by her streaming dreadlocks, the poor girl had clearly just suffered a terrific shock). In the same educational-cum-ornamental way, Eden may be said to represent the Spirit of Ecology. The plethora of placards may occasionally irritate, the (congested) road miles you have to drive to reach it can't be terribly eco-friendly and in high summer the heat for some might prove unsustainable. But the message is uncompromisingly effective, and you can't help but take away with you some searching questions and salutary truths about the diverse and endangered nature of our planet.

OPPOSITE, CLOCKWISE FROM TOP LEFT Nicholas Grimshaw's iconic hexagonal ETFE pillows; the approach to the 'biggest greenhouse on the planet'; prairie planting at the entrance to the Rainforest Biome; a colourful ribbon of herbaceous perennials; Eve reclining among silver birches in Wild Cornwall; inside the Mediterranean Biome.

LEFT Tree branches strung together with ropes climb the hillside behind the biomes, creating an eco-friendly stairway.

OVERLEAF Set in a disused china clay pit the size of thirty-five football pitches, with a Humid Tropics Biome that could hide the Tower of London, the Eden Project has been softened and transformed as the diverse and imaginative plantings cocooning the man-made structures increase and mature.

RIGHT One of the two yew walks planted at Tregrehan by W.A. Nesfield in the mid-nineteenth century have fused into vaulted roofing as sombre and numinous as that in a cathedral nave. They are set at right angles, with the longer run marking the transition from the productive and ornamental plantings near the house to the wooded valley at the perimeter. The shorter stretch runs to meet it from the formal parterre garden also created by Nesfield.

OPPOSITE The rose adorning a modest wooden door in the kitchen garden was collected by a friend of Tom Hudson from an old lady's garden in Lijiang, Yunnan.

Tregrehan

Of the two dozen gardens in this book, Tregrehan ranks very high indeed for all-round quality. The only thing it lacks is a coastal frontage, for the 100-acre estate lies a little way inland, surrounded by its park and woods and by agricultural land; it is separated from Carlyon Beach by the A390, and there are eighty-two steps down from the clifftop scrubland to the white-gold sand of the beach. The medieval deer park was Reptonized in the early nineteenth century and in the 1880s a lime avenue was planted to begin the sweep up to the handsome double-pile house (built around 1680 but given a classical coating by George Wightwick in 1842), where wisteria is trained low under the front windows and impressive clipped yew hedges flank the front door and its circular carriage sweep.

The largely level land on which sit the house and the adjoining group of working buildings is more generous than in many Cornish gardens of its type, for it extends well beyond the 1¼-acre walled kitchen garden next to the old grain mill and apple store, only starting its descent to the valley floor when it reaches the parallel yew walk that forms the main north–south axis across the entire width of the garden. This was not designed as an *allée* beckoning you to walk the paths of the woodland triangle stretching westwards; rather it is a barrier that must be crossed. It is interesting too that although these further reaches of the garden are by their very nature wilder and more informal, you are subconsciously aware that balance and geometry exist here also. Partly this is because of the lie of the land, partly because of the way the lie has been used and planted: there have clearly been thoughtful minds at work here.

Tom Hudson, Tregrehan's current owner, believes that the yew walk – or rather walks, for there is a shorter one running at right angles below the 1920s sunken garden on the south side of the house – was planted by William Andrews Nesfield, an influential but now largely forgotten designer of the 1840s–60s. His style, with its scalloped parterres and tailored shrubberies (he himself described it as 'artistical'), is at the other end of the spectrum from the Robinsonian style, which eschewed formal schemes in favour of natural-looking combinations of hardy perennials, shrubs and climbers. For Tregrehan Nesfield created a clipped centrepiece for the courtyard in front of the house and a parterre (eradicated now save for the statues of the Four Seasons that once pointed up the design) on the south side. His 1843 *parterre de broderie* pre-dated by more than a decade the one that formed a small part of his 'monster work'

BELOW Nesfield's fountain
lies at the heart of the
quadripartite kitchen garden,
backed by burgundy-coloured
Acer palmatum.

at Witley Court, where he also conjured up for the 1st Earl of Dudley a truly monstrous Perseus and Andromeda fountain; the noise it made as it was being fired up sounded to contemporary railway-age onlookers remarkably like an express train. For the kitchen garden at Tregrehan he had to make do with what is in effect a circular dipping pool, ornamented by a modest cherub and dolphin fountain.

Nesfield's surviving scheme for the kitchen garden has been overtaken by later touches of drama. The quadrants laid out with fruit, vegetable and picking flowers have been grassed over and planted with specimen trees and shrubs, the formal double border lining the path replaced by white roses confined by clipped box edging. The main corridor from the entrance is now flanked by two ravishing avenues planted in 1993: *Cornus capitata* to the central pool (terminated by a fireback of flaming acers), *Cordyline australis* to the gleaming 128-foot/39-metre line of glasshouses on the back wall. Barns and a dairy, partly

derelict now but still ornamental and built of charmingly pink slatestone, occupy the east wall.

While Nesfield helped shape part of the bones of the garden, successive owners contributed mightily to its planting. The estate has been in the same family since 1565, supported by a fortune based on mining that reached its peak during the Industrial Revolution. Colonel Edward Carlyon employed Nesfield during the 1840s and bought from the Veitch nursery near Exeter a quantity of trees collected by the Lobbs and rhododendrons collected by Joseph Hooker, but it was his grandson Jovey forty years later who formed the nucleus of the collection, praised by other horticulturists including Professor Charles Sprague Sargent of the Arnold Arboretum and W.J. Bean of Kew. In the 1960s Gillian Carlyon added camellias to the portfolio, hybridizing a significant number for a designated plantation adjoining the walled garden, adding others to the lawn in the walled garden and scattering a fair few in the woodland garden.

LEFT ABOVE *Magnolia wilsonii* shows off its pure-white, pendant blooms in summer.

LEFT BELOW The multi-branched coppery trunk of two *Rhododendron* 'Penjerrick' along a fern-fringed path, strewn with white blossom, in the upper reaches of the valley garden.

BELOW Bluebells have spread beneath a curtain of *Betula pendula* on the outer edge of the valley garden.

BOTTOM *Tsuga heterophylla* growing out of the rotting trunk of a Monterey pine that was struck by lightning.

RIGHT Sheep graze the turf at the parkland's edge in front of the house, where a layered bank of trees is fringed by azaleas and rhododendrons.

RIGHT Bluebells have spread in their thousands in the patch of deciduous woodland on the northern edge of the valley.

Tom Hudson, Gillian's cousin, is from the New Zealand branch of the family. He arrived at Tregrehan in 1987 and has been expanding the collection to suit himself and the Cornish climate with species from South-east Asia, Mexico, Tasmania, New Zealand and the southern regions of South America. He wears his knowledge and enthusiasm lightly, describing his huge involvement as a personal interest and his introductions as having been organized on an informal scientific basis with a lot of help from individuals and institutions. In the main garden he has done a considerable amount of planting, which includes specimen trees as companions to a misshapen but sculpturally riveting cedar by the tennis court, and created a new box design on the east side of the house. His heart, however, lies in the woodland garden, where he is replacing, augmenting and underplanting a century and more of tree-planting programmes in a new planting scheme based on phytogeographic zones.

It is a wonderful place, dark and cool but full of colour and opening out in the bowl at the bottom to a grassy floor and a conifer-ringed pond. The 400-year-old native and exotic trees are not just a shelterbelt, they are all-pervasive. And they and the newcomers are fascinating to dendrologists and ignoramuses alike. You might come upon a grouping of *Chamaecyparis pisifera*, *Pinus banksiana*, *Sequoiadendron giganteum*, *Podocarpus matudae*; walk through a carpet of fallen rhododendron petals; pass a stand of bamboo at one level or of tree ferns at another; ford the stream over the little blue bridge; look across the open floor from the tip of the triangle; or be drawn to a plantation of deciduous trees by the haze of bluebells at their feet. A gate at the top leads you back into the ghost of Nesfield's parterre, now firmly and permanently a swimming-pool garden. That is when you realize that not only the valley but the whole garden is breathing again, with a rhythm that is both deep and steady.

BELOW A pond with a grassy surround has been dug out of the valley floor; it is ringed by conifers, and swamp cypresses and other trees planted after 1989 are starting to establish themselves.

LEFT By the path from the yard to the Sunken Garden below the house, the bright pink flowers of *Cercis siliquastrum* are underplanted with box balls, a phormium and a splash of *Euonymus fortunei* 'Emerald 'n' Gold'; behind the beech hedge the *leylandii* hedge shutting out the car park is kept rigorously trimmed.

OPPOSITE A delicate composition of *Deutzia* x *hybrida* 'Mont Rose', artemisia and forget-me-nots is an eye-catcher along a border leading to the marsh.

Marsh Villa

In the eighteenth century the 3-acre triangle, roughly the same shape as India, that is Marsh Villa's garden – stretching north-eastwards from the house and barn positioned at its tip – lay well under water. It was and remains a site with an *über*-Cornish history. Tidal creeks then seamed the area, so that pilchards were seined in the valleys while miners extracted copper from the nearby Lanscot hills. Nature and industry continued to evolve side by side in the landscape: the valley decomposed into swampland, and as the pits closed the railway steamed in. Now the garden is constricted on its longest length by the main train line from Penzance to Paddington and on the other by a busy road, while an unobtrusive wooden gate on the perimeter furthest from the house leads into the 14 acres of untamed marshland known as Treesmill Marsh. Judith Stephens and her husband Harvey, tree planter, forester and labourer-in-chief, have spent twenty-five years making a remarkably interesting garden on this most unpromising site.

Few gardeners can have faced such a combination of challenges, including severe and prolonged annual flooding and tons of compacted household rubbish, not to mention the constant dirt and din of the trains. A flood-relief scheme, the manic deployment of crowbars and pickaxes, and a line of Leyland cypresses helped to overcome these major drawbacks, but even after the disaster zone had been worked into something resembling a meadow, it took all the couple's stamina and ingenuity to turn it into anything approaching a garden. The work involved was back-breaking. Where other gardeners can make do with the odd bag of compost, in order to make any impact at all on their barren and compacted soil they spent years raking up tons of countryside leaves, dredging rivers, digging neighbours' gardens for spare soil and cleaning out other friends' cattle yards.

'Gluttons for punishment' comes to mind, but they are rather characterized by a refusal to be beaten by nature, as well as possessing and maintaining standards that are both pragmatic and rigorous. The Sunken Garden is so called because it was excavated 8 feet/2.5 metres down to bring it level with its surroundings. The sizeable pond was dug far enough down to make sure the water level didn't drop below 4 feet/1.25 metres in summer; even Judith admits it cannot be described as labour-saving. Nor is the most recent project, the removal of a 100-foot/30-metre-long escallonia hedge and its replacement by a yew hedge and a herbaceous border.

LEFT Encouraged to press against a wooden bench, *Clematis* 'Guernsey Cream' is trained up a trellis in the Square Garden, the herbaceous summer garden adjoining the 14-acre Treesmill Marsh.

BELOW Throughout the garden, grass or gravel paths wind invitingly, and openings and enclosures are glimpsed through trees and along vistas. In the foreground, a curve of white and golden shrubs is topped by *Malus* x *zumi* 'Golden Hornet'; the raised bed on the left is planted with low-growing alpines.

In the end, however, far from proving a drawback, the quasi-industrial, quasi-wild nature of the site has made the garden a unique and marvellous place. The essentially informal nature of the design and planting is given structure by straight grass vistas, long hedges and a hornbeam avenue underplanted with hydrangeas *en bloc*. There are some formal areas too, but this garden is above all an expression of sheer delight in plants. There are unexpected combinations to enjoy: imagine, for example, the flaming clash of scarlet and lime green as you come upon *Lychnis coronaria* growing among *Euphorbia schillingii*. Colour combinations are now strong, now subtle: *Cotinus coggygria* 'Royal Purple' and *Berberis* x *thunbergii* 'Golden Ring' are stationed in front of the barn, the yellow fruits of *Malus* x *zumi* 'Golden Hornet' partnered for autumn with an eye-catching curtain of *Acer rubrum* 'October Glory'.

All over the garden beds and borders are bursting with specimen trees, shrubs of value and unusual perennials, and others are tucked wherever space permits, and everywhere favourite trees – on the southerly side *Sequoia sempervirens*, *Ginkgo biloba*, *Paulownia tomentosa*, *Catalpa bignonioides* 'Aurea' and *Taxodium distichum* – compete for space and light. Magnolias, cornus, osmanthus, shrub roses, eucryphias and exochordas shelter beneath them, with anemones, heucheras, violas, hostas and bulbs carpeting the ground. Essentially this is an ornamental woodland garden with borders, and now that the plantings in the separate areas have met, matured and married, the tapestry effect in spring and summer is both dense and subtle.

The map provided is prescriptive as to route. Visitors are invited to start near the house with a trio of small spaces with the homely names of Apple Tree Patch, Sunken Garden and the Frying Pan ('a fairly small frying pan'), and then strike out along the path that runs between a mixed border and a patch of ornamental woodland walk next to the railway line. When they reach the gate they can branch outside the garden to explore a little bit of the marsh (optional, this); then head for home through the herbaceous garden adjacent to the marsh and circling the pond to end with tea and plant purchases in the barn.

BELOW A long line of granite rocks overlooked by a swamp cypress separates paths leading off right and left to different parts of the garden. Planted with dwarf conifers and a range of spilling perennials and foliage plants, the scheme is currently being simplified to bring out the shapes and textures of the boulders.

ABOVE Near a bog garden, signalled by a flourish of *Gunnera manicata*, a grove of poplars has ground cover of hamamelis, hostas, astrantias and alchemilla, and three stone mushrooms.

OPPOSITE A trio of *Betula utilis* var. *jacquemontii* at the edge of the 2-acre pond, fringed by shrubs. The weeds on the water's surface are dragged out every autumn.

I'd rather deviate a little from this itinerary so as to make a beeline for the three most individually exciting parts of the garden. From the railway path I'd backtrack to the pond fringed with 'a motley mix' of plants that's large enough for a rowing boat to float on with plenty to spare. Then, crossing the only sizeable patch of lawn in the whole place, I'd head for an eye-catcher set in lawn among the trees – a formal herbaceous garden that stands out in its woodland surround with the same feeling of unreality as Hansel and Gretel's gingerbread house. The Square Garden (well, it is almost square) must break several cardinal rules, for although it is in many ways the heart of the garden, it is as far from the house as it could be, banged up against the perimeter wall that keeps the marsh at bay.

Here, within the new yew hedge are perennial borders that sublimate the extrovert in every garden designer. The central bed in August is massed with giant fennel, *Inula magnifica*, *Achillea*

grandifolia, echinops, macleayas and eupatoriums reaching heights of 8 feet/2.5 metres around a central support spilling over with *Lathyrus latifolius*. Annuals are plentifully scattered to inject later colour, and side borders are equally exuberant, one planted with hot-coloured flowers and foliage, the other with shades on the blue side of the spectrum. Adding to the theatrical effect is the fact that while the Square Garden is flat, it is overlooked to the north by a group of ornamental trees on a grassy bank.

The final element not to be missed is a foray into the one acre of Treesmill Marsh that's navigable on foot. The willows and alders that long pre-date the garden look down on islets of reeds and ferns and wild flowers, while herons, egrets and kingfishers flash among the dragonflies and damsel flies, and roe deer, badgers, foxes and otters have all been spotted picking their way along the streams. A place of utter peace.

Heligan

During the 1990s, the bringing-back of an intact and decomposed family estate by three private individuals, energized institutions and an army of volunteers became the stuff of legend, thanks to the romance of the story and a deftly orchestrated marketing campaign. Twenty-two years on, now that the newsworthiness has lost its cutting edge, Heligan is still a fascinating piece of horticultural history and a most interesting garden.

Tim Smit may have been the key agent of resurrection, but the Tremaynes, landowners from the mid-sixteenth century who fashioned the estate over three centuries, have rightly been kept at the heart of the account. Their 1,000-acre Cornish holding stood at the head of a valley above the historic fishing village of Mevagissey. The present red-brick house (William and Mary in front, Regency behind) and its grounds were serviced by a virtual township of craftsmen and labourers, and the estate seems always to have been run with enlightened and imaginative husbandry.

In 1766 Henry Hawkins Tremayne was pursuing a younger son's traditional calling as a local curate (and, one would like to think, a sporting parson in the best eighteenth-century tradition) when the property jigsaw was suddenly rearranged in his favour and, like Squire Allworthy in *Tom Jones*, he was 'decreed to the inheritance of one of the largest estates in the county' – actually in two counties, because he also came into possession of the Devon branch's estate in Sydenham. The 'plan of intended alterations for Hilligan the Seate of the Rev. Mr. Tremayne' drawn up by Thomas Gray after 1780 provided for the ornamental plantations and rides and the extensive and elaborate kitchen and cutting gardens appropriate to his new station.

The tripartite kitchen gardens – always the hub of the place – are spread over 2 acres, and bring together the ideas and developments of generations of horticulturally active Tremaynes. The largest and most utilitarian enclosure, furthest from the house, is the vegetable garden; built to an unusual trapezoid design, it is filled with long, impeccably maintained rows of vegetables, fruit and flowers. Next comes the nerve centre: the forcing ground or frameyard, where prized delicacies were encouraged into premature development by the use of heated beds and pits. Melons were first grown in England in the late sixteenth century, and at Heligan the frameyard, separated from the vegetable garden by a distinctive curving wall, is still called by its Tudor name, the melon yard. The pineapple pit is a late-eighteenth-century feature, while the elaborate network of bee

boles on the outside wall was built *c.*1820. The third element, separate from the first two, is the irregularly shaped walled fruit and flower garden nearest the house, surrounded by tall trees and mature rhododendrons. Here citrus, vine and peach houses have been angled to catch the sun, blocks of flowers are confined within substantial box compartments, and paths meet at a central circular dipping pool.

After Squire Henry's death, these productive gardens gained an outer ring of ornamental pleasure gardens created to display plants newly introduced from the Himalayas, New Zealand and Europe. Sir Joseph Hooker's mid-nineteenth-century expeditions to Nepal, Sikkim, Bhutan and Tibet (to which Sir Charles Lemon, Squire John Tremayne's brother-in-law, was a subscriber) resulted in the dispatch of some 150 rhododendrons

OPPOSITE, CLOCKWISE FROM TOP LEFT The melon yard with its frames and beautiful curving brick and stone wall; the Pencalenick Greenhouse on the edge of Sikkim; the bee bole wall outside the flower garden; clipped box compartments sheltering a crop of chives; work in progress along the regimented rows of the vegetable garden; the pineapple pit.

LEFT The impeccably clean and orderly toolshed was traditionally the head gardener's domain and the garden boy's bane – a place for everything and everything in its place. Note the stepped shelving, individual tool pegs and strings of flower pots hanging from the rafters.

RIGHT A handsome raised boardwalk leads across the topmost of the four ponds in the steep ravine valley known locally from its original planting after 1890 as the Jungle, passing clumps of bamboos, tree ferns, gunneras and waterlilies.

RIGHT Hidden away beside the melon yard, the Italian Garden – the last of the pleasure gardens to be designed, early in the twentieth century – is an intimate, semi-formal suntrap centred on a rectangular pool with a charming putto and dolphin statue, surrounded by olive trees, palms and a selection of Mediterranean plants.

and many camellias to Heligan (National Collections of both are held here). The fact that these pleasure gardens are integrated with the kitchen gardens rather than isolated from them in the usual fashion is key to the interest of the whole design.

One plant-hunter survivor is a vast *Rhododendron* Smithii Group sprawling on Flora's Green, north of the vegetable garden. With its grassy sward and generous supply of green benches, this large open space does indeed resemble a superior village green, surrounded by trees and a thick fringe of rhododendrons and camellias. Travelling clockwise beyond it comes a series of individual gardens emerging from a structural mesh of mature trees and shrubs. They are designed to show off the international range of the Tremaynes' interests and connections: the tree-fern-rich 'New Zealand'; the Sundial Garden with what was described in 1895 as 'the finest herbaceous border in the county'; 'Sikkim' and its Himalayan rhododendrons; a cool and secret Italian Garden; and the Ravine, originally intended to be the simulacrum of an alpine pass and now the ideal place for a collection of ferns.

These distinct ornamental areas are linked by looping paths and the two main rides that run from east to west the length of the productive gardens; poised along the route are carefully placed garden buildings. It is a complicated layout and has its own in-built clock: the summerhouse in the little garden on the south-eastern tip of Flora's Green catches the early morning sun, while the south-facing Italian Garden is a prime spot at midday, the west-facing Sundial Garden invites the last rays of the sun, and the grotto made of local crystal-veined rock on the eastern side can be candle-lit for winter-night celebrations.

Two valleys lying a distance from the house within the wider estate of agricultural and grazing land reveal another side of the Tremaynes. The Lost Valley is a working woodland with its own lake and mill pond which played a significant part in the day-to-day running of the estate. Adjoining it to the east, a steep-sided valley was transformed after 1890 into an interpretation of a Himalayan ravine, focused on a necklace of four linked ponds and lavishly planted with trees and shrubs imported from Asia, Australasia and the Americas. These neglected exotics, which included towering trees and significant collections of bamboos and tree ferns, soon rampaged away in their sheltered microclimate in a disorderly tangle referred to locally as the Jungle. They now been rescued, tamed and enhanced with new species, and the balance between wild and ornamental has been sensitively redressed.

Part of the excitement of Heligan as a story came from the onion-skin effect – the rolling-back of history, layer by layer, as buried buildings and smothered plantings resurfaced. Although the 'Lost Gardens' are lost no longer, having become instead something of a friendly, well-maintained, discreetly labelled and sophisticated 'experience', the feeling of adventure and discovery generated by Tim Smit and his fellow archaeologists persists.

BELOW The ivy-clad torso of the Mud Maid recumbent in a clearing off the woodland walk leading to the Jungle. One of three giant mud-and-plant sculptures created by local artists Sue and Peter Hill, she's an indication that Heligan is not just about restoration.

RIGHT The sycamore avenue on the eastern perimeter of the garden, adjoining the Horse Park. It runs the length of the Alison Johnstone Bay, named by the great plantsman George Johnstone for his wife and filled with a fine range of magnolias and some rare and exceptional trees and shrubs.

OPPOSITE The fuzzy-stemmed, intricately enamelled shepherd's crooks on the unfurling fronds of *Dicksonia antarctica,* planted in 1906. Very many of the tree ferns at Trewithen are to be found in the Cock Pit.

Trewithen

Trewithen does not have a dramatic coastal setting; nor was the garden consciously designed for theatrical effect. Although it has more than its fair share of rarities, including a superlative range of Asiatic magnolias, its collections of camellias and rhododendrons are not unsurpassed, and although it has twenty champion trees, that is only a quarter of the number at Caerhays. It is, however, a supreme gardener's garden, one that ranks among the best in the British Isles.

In 1738 a keen amateur dendrologist, Thomas Hawkins, inherited from his cousin Phillip a 28-acre estate lying midway between the county towns of Truro and St Austell. Aspiring to a garden to surround the cruciform house of which his predecessor had 'new built a great part' in order to be able to survey his park from every room, he laid out a 'pleasing labyrinth' of shelterbelt trees and radiating avenues which he further embellished with trees and flowering shrubs both native and foreign. This was the still pleasing but by then seriously overgrown canvas with which his descendant the great plantsman George Johnstone was confronted when he inherited the estate in 1904: 'It was necessary', he said delicately, 'to take an axe and claim air and light from amongst the trees, first for the house and those that should live in it, and then for the plants that must share the fortunes of the owner.'

Over the next forty-six years, until his death in 1960, Johnstone built up an internationally rated collection of trees and shrubs, many of them sourced from the wild by E.H. Wilson and George Forrest; the flood of new arrivals kicked off in 1905 with 100 hybrids of *Rhododendron arboreum*. Like J.C. Williams of Caerhays, he helped to sponsor Forrest's expeditions to China; he also planted at Trewithen many of Williams' famous *Camellia* x *williamsii* crosses, and the camellia walk includes species collected as seed by him in Palestine during the First World War, giving rise to *C.* 'Trewithen Red', 'Trewithen Pink' and 'Trewithen White'. The range of magnolias is even finer and more extensive, including a magnificent specimen of another of Forrest's introductions, a 65-foot/20-metre-tall *Magnolia campbellii* subsp. *mollicomata*. Cornwall's triumvirate – magnolias, camellias and rhododendrons – are therefore here in force, but they are well balanced for interest by a host of other rare and distinctive trees and shrubs, too many to list – some, like *Ceanothus arboreus* 'Trewithen Blue', bred by Johnstone.

Trewithen has been fortunate in the loyalty and longevity of its head gardeners, of which there have been just three in

BELOW When Thomas Hawkins rebuilt the handsome house in 1738, he gave it a suitably impressive setting of protective woodland, a landscaped park, radiating avenues and 'all sorts of English and Foreign plants'. His vision remains; his plantings have been further embellished by his descendants.

100 years (at Levens Hall in Cumbria the tally was ten in 300). Jack Stilton, who started estate life as a rook scarer, served sixty years; Mike Taylor, rhododendron and magnolia king who propagated many of the hybrids to be seen in the garden today, a mere forty. Gary Long, who took over in 2004, has miles to go before he sleeps.

Built of Pentewen granite, Trewithen is an imposing chameleon of a house, changing from grey to pink in the rain. The front façade has the simple grass-and-gravel carriage sweep ubiquitous in the period, and the garden proper thrusts out boldly from the rear. A broad and scalloped grass corridor – one of the very few tailored vistas in the whole garden – is flanked by layered plantings of trees and shrubs arranged in 'bays' named after Thomas Hawkins, Johnstone's wife Alison and J.C. Williams. Included among the superlative rhododendrons is R. 'May Day', raised by Williams at Werrington Park, and it is here too that the champion *Magnolia campbellii* subsp. *mollicomata* produces its astonishing leafless explosion of flowers in February and March.

The major surviving trees in the woodland garden at the end of this monumental ride were planted by Hawkins in the mid-eighteenth century; another big planting took place a century later. But while there has been continuous replacement of shelterbelt trees like podocarpus and *Pinus radiata*, and Johnstone's grandson Michael Galsworthy has planted thousands of trees, introducing new species such as eucalyptus and nothofagus, the main thrust remains Johnstone's eclectic choice of ornamentals. Galsworthy is following the tradition of using plants collected in the wild; where Johnstone availed himself of the services of George Forrest and E.H. Wilson, he turns to nurseries like Crûg Farm in Wales and Glendoick in Scotland. As before, the collection achieves some of the depth and concentration of a botanical garden without the scientific restrictions.

While in some woodland gardens controlled vistas and directional routes (and even, horror, intrusive signage) impel you onwards along a pre-ordained route, at Trewithen the articulation is kept deliberately fluid. Chipped-bark paths – recycled from the limbs and trunks of neighbouring trees – are restful on the eye and

feet, while the 'squints' chopped out of the dense understorey are an invitation to linger and wildlife corridors provide natural cross-routes. You can spend hours wandering among the rare and eye-catching species (*Hydrangea petiolaris* scrambling up to the topmost branch of an oak tree is an astonishing sight) without feeling any compulsion to consult a map, especially in spring, when the woodland bursts into bloom.

One delightful little enclave hidden on the northern boundary is peculiar to the garden – a dell, fashioned out of a quarry near the original ha-ha, which at one stage was used for cockfighting but was filled by Johnstone with ferns and tree ferns in one of his first mass plantings. The key months at Trewithen are spring to early July, but the year is held to start when the first flowers on *Magnolia sprengeri* open above the Cock Pit on 19 or 20 January – 'You could set your watch by it,' says Gary Long, except for 2010, when it was forty-seven days late. (The flowering year ends eleven months later with *Daphne bholua*.)

The twenty-first century has not seen the garden resting on its laurels – rather the reverse, as the dense plantations of that useful but invasive shrub that have grown up beneath the beeches in the woodland garden are being thinned out. The old walled garden – long given over to allotments – has been transformed into a rose garden in the shape of a Celtic cross, with an orchard of Cornish apples adjoining. The roses, planted in 2007–8 – pale colours on the shady side and hot on the sunny side – are pruned for shape in spring, and then pruned hard in October ('Otherwise they'd flower all year,' says Gary). New projects scheduled for 2012 are the creation of a pinetum in an outlying 10-acre field (this will feature worldwide specimens divided into climatic zones and underplanted with North American prairie plants), and the restoration of Hawkins' water garden in a valley north-west of the house.

At the heart of the garden are two touches of fantasy that might be seen as emblems of the garden: a contemporary version of that popular nineteenth-century device known as a *camera obscura*, which projects details of plants growing in the garden on to a table inside a raised 'hide'; and Tom Leaper's 1998 bronze magnolia flower, itself a symbol of Trewithen.

BELOW Seen from the house along the magnificent serpentine lawn, banks of rhododendrons, Asiatic magnolias and other spectacular flowering shrubs introduced by Johnstone are breathtaking in their spring plumage.

LEFT An astonishing sight among the roses and perennials in the summer garden planted in the former deer park: a superb specimen of *Cornus kousa* var. *chinensis*.

RIGHT ABOVE *Camellia* x *williamsii* 'Donation', one of many superior hybrids achieved by the serendipitous crossing of *C. saluenensis* and *C. japonica* by J.C. Williams of Caerhays (left). *Magnolia campbellii* is partnered by *Camellia* x *williamsii* 'Debbie' (right).

RIGHT BELOW The atmospheric Cock Pit, reputedly named for the cock fights that once took place here. Its cooler, damper microclimate has enabled ferns and tree ferns to flourish alongside magnolias and rhododendrons under a shady canopy that includes copper beech and *Acer maximowiczianum* (syn. *A. nikoense*).

Caerhays

'The sights that suddenly meet the eye are unforgettable. The visitor bursts in upon, not one or two, but a whole group of great Rhododendrons, trees rather than bushes, blazing with large trusses of magnificent flowers, white or pink or red. The whole planning has been carried out with masterly and at the same time unobtrusive skill, and the effects are often marvellous.' The Bishop of Truro was describing Caerhays at the turn of the twentieth century, when many of the plants flourishing there – commissioned by its owner from E.H. Wilson and George Forrest, from China and Japan – had never been seen in Europe before. Today's visitor may be familiar with all those exotic novelties, but the sights are still unforgettable, the effects marvellous. More perhaps than in any other Cornish garden except Trewithen, the contribution of one particular individual continues to make itself felt here.

In 1880 the eighteen-year-old John Charles Williams inherited the granite-grey castle built by John Nash about seventy years earlier, together with 100 acres of woodland and an estate that swallowed up all the secular land in the parish. Caerhays had been bought by his father, Michael, in 1854 after Hugh Trevanion – last in the line of a once-great county family,

related to the Edgcumbes of Cotehele and Mount Edgcumbe lived at Caerhays since the early fifteenth century – had fled the country to avoid bankruptcy, leaving behind him a house where one fascinated visitor found ducks 'washing themselves on the drawing room floor'.

Five years after inheriting Caerhays, 'J.C.' bought himself a house at Werrington – in the middle of the county, north of Launceston – and as his horticultural knowledge and interest deepened, he was able to make best use of the different soil and climate conditions in the two areas, dispatching new arrivals to the most favourable destination. The hardier species went to Werrington (whose greenhouses also grew orchids for Covent Garden market), those more appreciative of moist and misty conditions to Caerhays. In the eighteenth century the Cornish branch of the family had amassed a fortune in mining, smelting and banking, based at Burncoose House near Redruth, and this estate, twenty miles to the east, became a third repository of plants. Today it has taken on a modern plant-hunting role, sourcing plants for Caerhays from all over the world.

For the following six decades Williams was the very model of a modern country squire: MP, Lord Lieutenant three decades

BELOW Approached from the north, the castle was intended to reveal itself *seriatim*; on arrival, the coastal landscape is suddenly exposed in all its drama, as the land drops down to a large lake dotted with islands, a stretch of dunes and the sea beyond Porthluney, with a line of cliffs dominating the horizon.

RIGHT There has been a house on the present site since 1400. In the centuries that followed it was progressively aggrandized. In 1807 John Nash was called in to transform it into a castellated villa of considerable originality – and unsustainable expense.

later, benefactor to the National Trust and the Council for the Preservation of Rural England, promoter of local commercial horticulture. He was seemingly a man of few – though usually telling – words, and robust with it (the Bishop of Truro noted, in his obituary of Williams, that 'in a turbulent political meeting he could always get a hearing and when heckled he was at his best').

More importantly for Caerhays, he was also a collector and hybridizer, highly regarded in the horticultural profession. Famously he crossed *Camellia saluenensis* with *C. japonica* to produce the x *williamsii* hybrids, but he would also make dozens of new rhododendron crosses each year, and his work with magnolias was legendary. Between 1885 and the 1930s these three, together with daffodils and fuchsias, claimed his attention, but the range of plants he collected far exceeded these few species. It is worth listing some of those mentioned in the Bishop's obituary to give an idea of plants considered worthy of being planted at Caerhays: *Prunus conradinae* and *P. mume*, *Acer griseum*, *Staphylea holocarpa*, *Tetracentron sinense*, *Nothofagus obliqua*, *Betula albosinensis* var. *septentrionalis* and *B. utilis*, several species of styrax and evergreen oaks, *Magnolia doltsopa* (syn. *Michelia doltsopa*), several varieties of

Within a protective cordon of shelterbelt trees a wealth of exotic and unusual plants, including many rare in Cornwall, are often associated together in groups, creating their own microclimate on the sloping ground – here *Rhododendron* 'High Sheriff' and a pair of award-winning *R.* 'Tinner's Blush'.

peony, *Meliosma veitchiorum*, *Gordonia axillaris*, *Erica australis* f. *albiflora* 'Mr Robert' (after J.C.'s son, killed during the First World War); *Corylopsis pauciflora*; *Rosa moyesii*, *Escallonia* 'Iveyi', several species of primula, clematis and lonicera. The story runs that a prominent French horticulturist on a tour of Cornish gardens, having visited Caerhays, was seen to abandon his usual practice of taking copious notes with which to impress his peers back home. Asked why, he replied: 'But it is impossible, for they will no longer believe me.'

In the eighteenth century the Caerhays house had been surrounded by its working buildings and outhouses, kitchen gardens, orchards and nurseries, flower garden and wilderness, lawns and parkland. Although it lay on higher ground than the present dwelling, it was still dismissed by Thomas Tonkin in the 1720s as being 'too much under a hill'. Nash sited his castle looking south-eastwards across a lake towards the curve of Veryan Bay. Unlike similar estates such as Glendurgan and Trebah – and although in 1853 Michael Williams made 'the great cut' through the hillside to promote the view – the main

focus of interest is not the sea view but rather the heavily planted woodland rising on the other three sides.

The garden behind the house is surrounded by farmland fields; then come two outer clumps of woodland – Old Park Wood and Forty Acre Wood. Within the rim of shelterbelt trees on the western and southern flanks is an inner windbreak – the substantial laurel hedge planted along the hillside was by Williams' death in 1939 some 30 feet/9 metres tall, and laurels were also scattered to form glades within the woodland. The intimate groupings within these sheltered enclaves can be charming: *Acer palmatum* var. *dissectum* grouped with *Kalopanax septemlobus* (syn. *K. pictus*), the bristly-hipped chestnut rose *Rosa roxburghii* and *Magnolia sargentiana* var. *robusta*, for example; or *Acer henryi* rubbing shoulders with *Quercus lamellosa* and *Magnolia* 'Philip Tregunna' (bred at Caerhays and named for its then head gardener).

There is a style favoured by many plantsmen that is sometimes rudely dismissed as 'yoghurt-pot gardening' – an obsessive amassing of the rare and unusual with little regard for

LEFT Another, yet more colourful, trio: *Rhododendron* 'High Sheriff', the darker pink *R.* 'Sir Charles Butler' and the deep lavender *R.* 'Saint Tudy'.

ABOVE LEFT *Magnolia* 'Star Wars'.
ABOVE RIGHT *Magnolia*
x *soulangeana*.
OPPOSITE *Magnolia* x *veitchii*
'Peter Veitch' by the entrance to
the garden.

design or colour blending. J.C. Williams, although a passionate collector, was not a twitcher and his plantings were finely tuned to the aesthetics of the site (he favoured the widest possible distribution of the plants he raised and bred, demanding only that the recipients like and not merely want them).

Caerhays is essentially all about discovery and display – especially of rhododendrons, magnolias and camellias never before seen in Europe during Williams' day and now achieving colossal heights. To encounter specimens in full bloom along the woodland walks and at virtually every turn of the path is astonishing. If he were aiming to replicate one of the tumbling landscapes of south-west China captured on camera by George

Forrest, he succeeded. As well as notable collections of evergreen oaks and podocarpus, over eighty champion trees are distributed through the garden, not only camellias and rhododendrons but unusual species such as *Aesculus wilsonii* and *Acer forrestii*. One imagines the two men for whom these were named finding themselves unable to resist adding such unknowns to their trophies as they combed the hillsides for their patron.

At Caerhays the alternative routes are well signposted, the plants exceptionally well labelled. It is almost impossible to leave the garden without being brushed, however faintly and fleetingly, with the pure spirit of enquiry, research and dissemination of knowledge that drove J.C. Williams and his successors.

Lanhydrock

The story of the Robartes, barons and earls and lords of Lanhydrock for nearly four hundred years, is marked by misfortune – spinster sisters and heirs without issue, untimely deaths, absentee landlords. The house first remodelled by Baron Robartes of Truro in 1625 was likewise a sad place: one of the few people to visit in the mid-seventeenth century, the Reverend William Borlase, noted that the house was not only 'in a state of neglect and decay' but boasted just one picture, 'and that a bad one'. The park, he found, 'has great variety of up and down Wood, some fine and scattered trees and lawns, but the spine is cold, black and ferny'.

The succession was to sidestep its way down the generations, and the first of a bewildering number of name changes occurred when the Baron's son John was made Earl of Radnor and Viscount Bodmin by Charles II. He and his successors tinkered with renovations and repairs, but it was Thomas Agar Robartes (a long-time MP for East Cornwall, he had been proud to add the name of his estate to his title, becoming the 1st Baron Robartes of Lanhydrock and Truro), who was responsible for the basic layout of the gardens in the mid-nineteenth century. In 1881 the house was virtually destroyed by fire; within days the shock had claimed the life of its chatelaine, and her husband died the following year. The family was clearly resilient, however: his heir, later Viscount Clifden, immediately commissioned

BELOW A double beech avenue leads up to the gatehouse, giving a stunning impression of the complex of buildings; the approach now, however, is along a path running parallel to the gatehouse wall. Behind rises woodland planted as a shelterbelt for the house and the Higher Garden.

RIGHT The view from the Higher Garden reveals the house (rebuilt after a fire in 1881) as a roofscape adorned with an astonishing number of chimneys. It's also a reminder of the spacious park and rolling landscape that lie outside the ornate formal and pleasure gardens that surround the house.

RIGHT The twin octagonal towers of the mid-17th-century gatehouse, topped by crenellated parapets and obelisks, are a suitably dominant backdrop for the clipped Irish yews marking the corners of the six flower beds set into the terraced lawns in front of the courtyard.

RIGHT In the ornate geometric parterre on the north side of the house, begonias and busy Lizzies confined within clipped box shapes compose a traditional Victorian summer bedding scheme. The fine 17th-century bronze urn is one of a set formerly at the Château de Bagatelle in Paris.

a local architect, Richard Coad – who had already worked at Lanhydrock under George Gilbert Scott – to rebuild the house with modern improvements; his interiors were felicitously described by John Cornforth as 'the first house I have seen where equal attention is given to both sides of the green baize door'. In 1953 the 7th Viscount signed over house, 30-acre gardens, park and woodlands to the National Trust.

The impressive and highly decorative seventeenth-century gatehouse, topped by ball finials and crenellated parapets, which marks the main eastern entrance to the house, is approached along a double beech avenue planted in 1827 to replace the original 1648 single avenue of sycamores. Nowadays the impact of the avenue is muted, for visitors first catch sight of it and the gatehouse sideways on, but the formal garden laid out in 1857 on the three lawned terraces on the east side of the house matches it for drama. The original plan was drawn up by the London architect George Truefitt, executed and adapted by Coad: a geometric pattern of six flower beds filled with Floribunda roses, centred on the avenue and marked at each corner by clipped Irish yews, strong and sombre hulks that virtually people the space.

For the north side Truefitt devised an ornate parterre with colourful and disciplined blocks of tulips, pansies, begonias and busy Lizzies in clipped box compartments. Although perhaps not greatly to twenty-first-century taste, the whole composition, including the handsome bronze urns made by Claude Ballin, Louis XIV's goldsmith, is undeniably in tune with the rhythm of

the house and the fine and dominant crenellated and pinnacle wall erected by Coad to enclose this formal scheme.

Two 'political' copper beeches planted by William Gladstone and Lord Rosebery dominate the tennis lawn overlooking the parterre. On the far side of the parterre, also just outside this elegant stockade but forming an integral part of the house and its ancillary buildings, is the church of St Hydroc, set in its own mini-grounds; its tower commands the approach to the rest of the garden. The true character of Lanhydrock may really be said to lie not in the architectural and horticultural geometry of the artificially flattened formal garden but in the rising ground here, for the estate is situated on the western slope of the River Fowey 400 feet/123 metres above sea level – and the slope is steep.

Here, in the heart of the garden, the informal pleasure gardens created in the mid-nineteenth century sweep grandly away from the house. They are negotiated up a succession of steps or grassy slopes that break up the verticality of the site and give it a natural sense of direction. On the north-west of the house, a network of walks curves among trees and ornamental shrubs. In 1930 the 7th Viscount Clifden discovered this part of the garden to be 'Nothing but clumps of Portuguese Laurel', which he replaced with scores of fine and rare magnolias, joined now by an equally splendid range of rhododendrons, azaleas, camellias, eucryphias and specimen trees. Further to the south a broad path indicates the boundary with the Higher Garden.

LEFT The division between the formal gardens and the little church of St Hydroc is marked by an impressive crenellated wall built by local architect Richard Coad to reflect the strong lines of the gatehouse. The ornate ensemble of architectural statements is softened by roses and a bed of mounded lavenders.

RIGHT Behind a feathery wall of rodgersias in the pleasure grounds north-west of the house, the herbaceous circle stretching behind the wisteria-clad gable end of the tithe barn is planted with perennials, with *Iris sibirica* and *Actaea racemosa* standing out among a sea of green.

RIGHT In an intimate corner behind the church, with the clipped yews of the formal garden glimpsed in the background, a herbaceous border has been laid out beneath the spreading branches of *Magnolia campbellii*.

It is impossible to do justice to Lanhydrock's magnolias, which are scattered throughout the garden, but for magnificence it's perhaps not invidious to pick out *M. grandiflora* on the north wing of the house, and six others – three *M. campbellii* subsp. *mollicomata* and three *M. x veitchii* – in the pleasure gardens. Flowers range in colour from spectacular white *M.* 'Albatross' and pale pink *M. sargentiana* var. *robusta* to pale purple *M. x loebneri* 'Leonard Messel' and deep rose *M. campbellii* subsp. *mollicomata* 'Peter Borlase', named for and planted by a former head gardener. The flowering range is vast too; indeed it is claimed that at least one will be in flower every day from early March to December.

Take the path from the magnolia glade rising towards a tall and curving yew hedge, and you come to a graceful surprise: a circular flower garden filled by four wedge-shaped beds planted with herbaceous perennials. Two reflect the planting preferences of Lady Clifden, chatelaine in 1914, who chose for her design a mix of crocosmias, peonies, veronicas, fuchsias, dicentras, geraniums and other traditional favourites; the other two were planted by the Trust in 1972 with a more exotic character, using such things as crinums, agapanthus, schizostylis and ophiopogon. An outer path hugs the hedge line and an inner grass strip enables visitors to walk among the flowers.

As you climb on upwards along the broad straight path on the southern boundary of the pleasure gardens, there comes a second surprise – a low, dark, curving tunnel of *Magnolia x soulangeana* 'Lennei', which effectively marks the transition to the Higher Garden – the long and linear second band of plantings on the south-west and south sides of the house. Now the rhythm changes again: strides lengthen and the pace quickens as you forge along paths set in strips of mown grass past towering trees, mature shrubs and broad mixed borders embracing a wide range of shrubs, perennials and exotics. Beech, sycamore, oak, ash and sweet chestnut, interspersed with conifers and underplanted with rhododendrons, camellias and other ornamental shrubs, are the major trees in the woodland, which merges into the gardens at the upper level. They feature too in the encircling 200-acre park, formerly a deer park, which by the late eighteenth century had already been incorporated into the ornamental landscape.

The views towards Bodmin Moor, the Fowey Valley and Restormel Castle are very fine, the planting exuberant and historically interesting; and there are many architectural features to be discovered along the walks. But it is the house, splendidly set off by its jewelled setting, that remains in the mind even in the furthest, highest reaches of the Higher Garden.

LEFT Backed by a disciplined yew hedge, a cool and sophisticated herbaceous scheme is planted with ophiopogons, heucheras, alliums and irises in shades of black, claret, purple, pink and blue.

Bosvigo

Richard Carew, squire of Antony House near Torpoint on the far west side of the county, wrote in his 1602 *Survey of Cornwall* of the owners of the sturdy manor houses and farmhouses tucked away from the wind and rain punishing the rugged coastal strip that they 'keep liberal, but not costly builded or furnished houses, give kind entertainment to strangers, are reverenced and beloved of their neighbours, live void of actions amongst themselves'. These admirable men worked hard to harness the natural assets of the soil and the sea, and they played hard too. Carew paints a charming picture: 'A gentleman and his wife will ride to make merry with his next neighbour, and after a day or twain, those two couples will go to a third, in which progress they increase like snowballs, till through their burdensome weight they break again.'

The eponymous house built in the twelfth century high above Truro by Ypolitus de Bosuuego (who in spite of his glorious name had a fortune rooted in tin-smelting) may well have been one of those agreeably convivial dwellings. Later owners, especially the Georgians, added their individual architectural imprint, and now the abiding impression is of an elegant farmhouse with pretty Regency Gothic windows, a front hung with magnolias, clematis and jasmine and an interior made charming by old flagstones, intricate woodwork and a colossal kitchen dresser.

Some of the grand Cornish gardens – dominated by water and sky, with deep ravines and the dramatic coastline always in the mind's eye – seem almost to exist in isolation from their houses. Not so Bosvigo, where the garden knocks at every window. Forty years ago, when Michael and Wendy Perry arrived, it had shrunk to a single acre, but it doubled in size as, little by little, they clawed back further pockets of land. The unusual way the space is ordered behind the house harks back perhaps to those piecemeal purchases.

The entrance façade, fronted by a carriage sweep around a circular lawn, is traditional enough. To the right of the front door, entered through a gate in a wall next to the handsome Victorian greenhouse, is a small walled garden planted in pastel shades for summer and early autumn in memory of the Perrys' daughter Hannah, a victim of the 2004 tsunami. The wall opposite the entrance is hung with pale grey Cornish slates, a perfect complement to the thalictrums, campanulas, roses, geraniums and asters ordered in loose combinations below. By contrast, the Hot Garden on the other side peaks in late summer and early autumn with a potent combination of

crocosmias, salvias, lobelias, dahlias and dusky foliage. Layout and planting are not typically Cornish: close your eyes and you could be in the Cotswolds.

Bosvigo is unusual and memorable, not only for the skill of its planting but also for the curious, higgledy-piggledy nature of its architecture and landscaping – an affair of small enclosures and frequent changes of level. Odd it may be, but it works. Climbing the narrow, curving path leading round to the rear of the house, you find yourself on an elbow-hugging path leading to an entrance door at first-floor level, and looking down into a courtyard on either side. It transpires that the building on the left, the Vean, is a separate dwelling, acquired at a later date along with its own diminutive garden; this is now planted as a happy mixture of formal topiary shapes softened by perennials allowed to spill out as they please, with greens, greys and blues dominating.

Once you've given up trying to make sense of this 'Mary Ann' arrangement, you're drawn irresistibly on to circle round the house, hugging a steep bank crowned with an exclamatory *Acer palmatum* 'Sango-kaku' up to a summer house fronted by a russet-coloured berberis hedge, and then down again

ABOVE A froth of *Erigeron karvinskianus* associates with *Rosa* 'Raubritter' in a delicate wave of white and pink along the steps leading down into the Vean courtyard.

OPPOSITE Ringing the changes with surface textures and topiary is important in the confined areas surrounding the house; here a corner of the enclosed garden is visible through a doorway.

under gateways cloaked with climbers, past a pair of standard variegated elaeagnus in pots guarding a door set into the old wall, and through a seemingly endless succession of little enclosures. Each part of this diffuse and layered core is different in planting and atmosphere.

As a teenager Wendy Perry started an art course. She did not complete it, but her intense feeling for colour and design has stayed with her. She notices colours the way the compulsive housewife locks into cobwebs, and is also that rarity a plantswoman who not only loves plants and buys them compulsively from nurseries all over the country and from like-minded friends but is also able to position them with absolute certainty. She can also do lavish: the generous smattering of bulbs at the top of the garden makes the same *pointilliste* impact as the flowery meads of the Unicorn Tapestries. With characteristic self-deprecation, she ascribes her close attention to detail, evident everywhere, to her short sight, and says that it affects her attitude towards vistas too; she describes herself as an enclosed town gardener, constantly looking down and across narrow spaces. So views are short by choice, and besides there was never quite enough money to concentrate on the further-flung parts of the garden, for example the old tennis court, which are the best lookout points.

It is ultimately the range and variety of the planting that make a visit here unforgettable. It may be that if it were not in a sense a show garden, with a fully functioning nursery attached and a hellebore open day that is packed with cheerful but determined punters who are clearly veterans of the first day of the sales, a greater number of calm spaces might have been created. The woodland adjoining the narrow lane next to the entrance gates is certainly packed with plants, but it's hard to believe that calm is needed here – the intensive drifts of colour from the bulbs, perennials and shrubs spreading out under the sycamores and 100-year-old beech trees make for a multi-layered tapestry and an exhilarating wander.

Wendy Perry insists, surprisingly for one both knowledgeable and passionate about plants, that she's not a purist – she is happy to introduce the often-ridiculed ruby chard to fill a gap. She is also unsentimental about individual purchases and ruthless at chucking out those that fail to earn their keep. Bosvigo is a fine advertisement for tough love.

RIGHT A symphony in foliage colours in the garden fronting the Vean, a separate dwelling linked to the main house. The walls are hung with green and golden ivies, and clipped balls and pyramids reinforce the plantings surrounding the front door.

RIGHT The walled garden created in memory of daughter Hannah flames into flower in midsummer, with *Clematis* 'Madame Julia Correvon' and *Rosa* x *odorata* 'Mutabilis' adorning the wall above a border richly layered with berberis, sambucus, geraniums and a wealth of other plants.

LEFT A lovely specimen of the coral bark maple, *Acer palmatum* 'Sango-kaku', in the woodland walk, showing off its perfect habit of growth and marvellous range of leaf colour, which changes season by season, ending with pink winter shoots.

BELOW LEFT The contrasting flowers of *Gillenia trifoliata* and *Geranium sanguineum* 'Album' are perfectly set off by the soft and hairy leaves of the false forget-me-not *Brunnera macrophylla* 'Jack Frost'.

BELOW RIGHT Wendy Perry has an educated instinct for colour and rejoices when a single plant has it all, like this epimedium where green, red and white are interwoven in a dense but delicate mat.

RIGHT Standing on the summer-house bridge midway down the long and narrow slope, looking down on a gravel bed studded with succulents towards the trees and shrubs on the next level, is a dizzying experience.

OPPOSITE ABOVE The view through the archway positioned halfway up the flight of steps, which is the only straight axis in the garden. Beyond the statue of Flavia, overhung by *Trachycarpus fortunei*, the lower garden is dedicated to succulents and southern-hemisphere plants.

OPPOSITE BELOW At the lowest level of the garden, an airy, roofless cupola supported on slender Ionic columns stands on a terrace looking up to the sky and out to sea and St Anthony's headland. It is surrounded by palms and scented flowers.

Lamorran

The hanging garden of Lamorran rolls down to the sea, with glimpses of passing boats and of the lighthouse at St Anthony's Headland a reminder that trade and tourism carry on in the maritime world outside. Looking down from the house terrace, it seems at first sight a perfect 'Douanier Rousseau' jungle: a curtain of foliage punctuated by palms and tree ferns and flashes of vibrant colour – tigers must surely be lurking in the undergrowth, drinking from the many pools, streams and little waterfalls.

When in 1982 Robert and Maria Dudley-Cooke discovered the house and its 4.5-acre garden tucked away on the Roseland Peninsula north of St Mawes, an early interest in Japanese gardening and a growing enthusiasm for the plants and gardens of France, Spain and especially Italy shaped their intentions, and the warmth and wetness of this climatically blessed corner of Cornwall did the rest. The orientation is due south, the location the northern shore of the north-easternmost finger of the intricate inland waterway known as the Carrick Roads.

Lamorran is one of those gardens where it is important to get to grips with the layout before embarking on the zigzag network of paths that meet at a vantage point looking out to sea. On plan, the space is divided into four zoned bands dominated by subtropical vegetation and southern-hemisphere exotics and anchored into the steep site by architectural trees and shrubs, a complexity of paths and a vertical central stairway. The controlled vistas, landscaping and relaxed but disciplined planting bring back memories of Italy, evident too in the long flight of steps that moves the action progressively down towards the bay. Lawns, archways and bridges help to direct the downwards flow, while a plentiful smattering of urns and statues emphasizes vistas and changes of direction, and airy garden buildings enhance the Mediterranean atmosphere. (If anything could be said to deflect attention from the vitality and interest of the plantings, it might be the sheer number of these architectural flourishes.)

As is often the case in Cornwall, the house stands on the only flat surface available, at the head of the slope, and its immediate surroundings seem different in character from the main garden unfolding below. The walled garden next to the house is the one space that approaches formality. Here gravel paths and clipped topiary give structure to a range of Mediterranean plants: climbers such as *Jasminum polyanthum*, bougainvillea and mandevilla, and flowering shrubs including acacias, ceanothus, cistus and fuchsias. Below the broad house terrace adjoining,

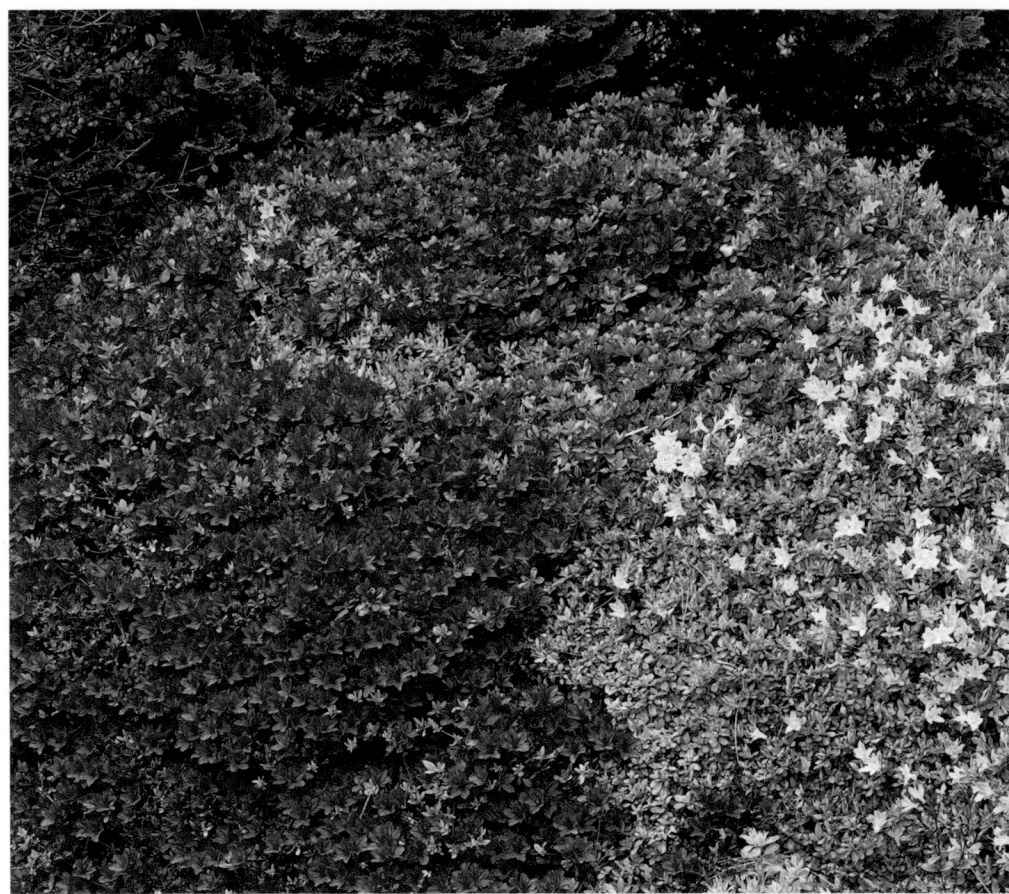

ABOVE LEFT White *Clematis armandii* is wrapped around a pale pink *Camellia reticulata* cultivar.

ABOVE RIGHT Throughout the garden, evergreen azaleas (here *Rhododendron* 'Amoenum') are cloud-clipped in summer to form distinctive mounds.

RIGHT The koi pool in the Japanese-inspired water garden lies between the entrance and the house, at the head of the network of paths threading their way through the garden's many layers. Cool, damp and dark, it is shaded by one of the tree ferns that, together with palms, are the signature plants of Lamorran.

with its citrus trees in pots and the first of the many palms, is a collection of ericaceous plants native to Cornwall.

Although plants are massed throughout the garden – and there's an enticing range here of both the rare and the familiar – the structure is informally disciplined. Foliage planting starts in earnest east of the terrace with a patch of woodland, and a little Japanese-inspired area of gravel paths and a pool with a waterfall, koi carp and stone lanterns. Concentrated plantings are fitted in at different levels, divided loosely into palms and tree ferns, Macaronesian plants and southern-hemisphere species, collections of banksias and proteas, puyas and agaves, cacti and succulents. Similarly, water runs through the garden in all its guises and at every level.

The garden as a whole is held together and given rhythm and continuity by a series of repeat plantings: *Luma apiculata*, yuccas, ceanothus, cistus, acacias, rhododendrons and azaleas. The trees are well chosen to fit this scheme: *Pinus radiata*, so often

used in Cornwall as a shelterbelt tree, *Xanthocyparis nootkatensis* 'Pendula' with its graceful cloak of branches reaching to the ground, *Cupressus sempervirens* 'Swane's Gold'. Dominating the whole are tree ferns (eighteen different species, especially of dicksonia and cyathea) and palms, some two hundred in all). Among the latter, 40-foot/12.25-metre-high *Trachycarpus fortunei* and handsome *Phoenix canariensis* contrast with the stubby, single-trunked *Chamaerops humilis* and its silver-leaved form, *C.h.* var. *cerifera*, while *Butia yatay*, the aptly named feather palm from South America, really does look like one of those boas wielded so dextrously by dancing girls.

Plants are massed here in enormous numbers. The narrowness of the paths means you're in constant contact with rare and familiar trees, bushes and flowers as they brush against or tower above you, while the steep slope requires concentration every step of the way. A visit to Lamorran is, therefore, an energetic and fully engaging experience.

BELOW Palms and tree ferns in a grassy clearing near the top of the garden, where *Dicksonia antarctica* and *Chamaerops humilis* come together with *Trachycarpus fortunei*, *Pittosporum tenuifolium* and *Acacia dealbata*. In the foreground, *Skimmia japonica* and *Rhododendron* 'Amoenum' trace the line of the gravel path.

Trelissick

Superlatives are easily invoked by anyone trying to pin down the spirit of Cornish gardens, but Trelissick invites them in multitudes. For a start, its setting – cradled by the River Fal as it winds round to spill into the Carrick Roads – is superbly panoramic. The numinously named Roads – actually a river valley flooded at the end of the last ice age – has a deep channel running through the centre of its filigreed outline that makes it navigable from Truro right down to Falmouth. Two other great gardens, Glendurgan and Trebah, make similar topographical use of the beautiful Helford River a loop or two further south, but the upper reaches of the Roads are Cornwall at its most intricate and intriguing.

In shape, the estate resembles an eccentric jigsaw piece, roughly triangular with a few awkward bits protruding. It has an ancient and complicated history. The name Trelesyck first cropped up in 1280, and over the centuries the habitation grew from a seventeenth-century farmhouse to a substantial early nineteenth-century country house described by Pevsner as 'the severest Neo-Greek mansion in Cornwall'. Unusually for this patriarchal part of the world, no one family controlled its fortune for very long; less unusually, their own fortunes oscillated markedly. The mid-eighteenth-century incumbent, John Lawrence, was known for his 'good nature, convivial habits and wild eccentricities'; after his death in 1790 his heir was bankrupted and the estate 'Peremptorily Sold'. It was bought in 1805 by Ralph Allen Daniell, whose mother was the niece and heiress of Ralph Allen of Prior Park in Bath and whose tin-mining interests made him allegedly the richest man in Cornwall. He continued to remodel the house and its surrounding 500 acres until his death in 1823, when his son Thomas, a notable *bon viveur*, inherited. Thomas was declared bankrupt nine years later.

As the nineteenth century ran its course, the estate was periodically bought, sold or let to a succession of unrelated owners – luckily, all horticultural enthusiasts who established a legacy of tree-planting that is the backbone of Trelissick today. They laid out the basic structure of enclosures, walks and pleasure grounds, and invested in exotics, enthusiasm for which was sweeping county and country. Carew Davies Gilbert, an avid traveller and

Trelissick stands at the mouth of the River Fal, and the garden's panoramic views stretch across the Carrick Roads, a vast natural harbour formed during the Ice Age.

BELOW LEFT A wisteria in fine
flower cloaks the brick wall
along the entrance walk leading
to the King Harry Ferry. The twin
roofs of the conical 1820s water
tower are in the background.

plant collector in the Americas, Japan and southern Europe and a fan of William Robinson's style of wild gardening, was especially active during the latter years of the century.

In 1937 Ida Copeland inherited the estate from her stepfather, Leonard Daneham Cunliffe, a former Governor of the Bank of England, and with her husband set about the mammoth task of replanting the main garden. Roland Copeland was managing director of the Spode china company, which produced a series of dinner and tea services in 1947 engraved with 'Rhododendrons seen at Trelissick', following this up with 'Camellias seen . . .' and 'Birds seen . . .'. The 376-acre estate, including its park, woodland and garden, was made over to the National Trust in 1955. Copelands still live in the house and enjoy its stupendous views.

The house is set in the middle of parkland, created from farmland in the mid-eighteenth century, developed and restocked over the centuries, and replanted by the Trust with oak, sycamore,

sweet chestnut, ash and larch. The impressive front portico looks out over it, and it also forms the backdrop to the house looking upwards from the river. It suffers, however, the fate of many coastal parks in being just that – a backdrop – for the views are focused on the Roads, and it is to the south and east that Trelissick's walks and ornamental gardens stretch out.

The original productive areas are located nearest the house. First come three enclosed spaces: the diminutive Fig and Parsley Gardens, and a 2-acre walled kitchen garden. This was formally laid out in the mid-eighteenth century in a pattern of standard fruit trees interspersed with soft fruit and vegetables, with other fruit trees trained against the walls. In the late nineteenth century Trelissick was known as the fruit garden of Cornwall, and Ronald Copeland extended the range with peaches, nectarines and figs; enough produce was delivered to the cooks to feed some twenty-five people daily until the 1930s. Currently, however,

the kitchen garden is a blank and grassy canvas, awaiting restoration funds.

Across the lane leading to the King Harry Ferry, reached via a decorative timber bridge, lies a separate area known as Carcaddon. This was planted as an orchard in the 1960s, and although now replanted as an arboretum of specimen trees and conifers arranged in grassy glades and underplanted with groups of ornamental shrubs and drifts of daffodils, it still remains orchard-like in character. The western end has been laid out by the Trust, quincunx-style, with an important collection of Cornish apples – 'Cornish Gilliflower', 'Lady's Finger', 'Pig's Snout', 'The Rattler', 'Tregonna King' and some ninety other enticingly named cultivars.

Overall, as with Carcaddon, the present plantings are relatively recent in Cornish terms, dating from the mid-twentieth century onwards, with a focus on Asiatic species. In the upper part of the main gardens, where long paths lope through shrubberies carpeted with bulbs, wild flowers and perennials, Ronald Copeland still casts a long shadow. He planted for present enjoyment, favouring hybrid rhododendrons, azaleas, camellias and hydrangeas, and the Trust has extended the range with collections of azaras and photinias and increased the number of summer-flowering shrubs and perennials, including unusual hydrangeas, willow gentians and *Impatiens tinctoria*.

In the lower part, near the bridge that crosses over the road leading to the King Harry Ferry and carries on into Carcaddon, are three contrasting areas. The pretty hydrangea walk, where the blooms, ranging from white to pale blue and the very dark blue *H. macrophylla* 'Enziandom', are overhung with flowering cherries and underplanted with drifts of narcissi and bluebells, was Copeland's idea too. The neighbouring dell, replanted by the Trust, is exotic in feel, with bananas (sheltering the rarely

BELOW CENTRE *Acer palmatum* 'Seiryu' backed by a prunus in Carcaddon, a former orchard and nursery absorbed into the wider garden in the 1960s and planted with an eclectic collection of ornamental trees and large shrubs.

BELOW RIGHT A fretwork of spring blossom combines *Prunus* 'Kanzan' and *Magnolia* x *soulangeana* 'Rustica Rubra'.

seen *Schefflera rhododendrifolia* from South Africa), tree ferns, bamboos, cannas and hedychiums; and a boggy area fed by natural drainage has marsh marigolds, skunk cabbages and *Gunnera manicata*.

At the heart of Trelissick is a large lawn, dominated by a *Cryptomeria japonica* planted in 1898, that slopes gently down from the main path towards Carcaddon. As at Heligan, *Rhododendron* Smithii Group (Copeland's favourite) looms on one side, and deep and curving mixed borders are planted for spring, summer and early autumn with a marvellous array of trees, shrubs and herbaceous plants: cool colours facing east, hot facing south, with subtropical specimens for added height and drama. This is the Trust at its imaginative best.

OPPOSITE ABOVE The decorative modern timber footbridge leading into Carcaddon across the lane to the ferry is hung with white wisteria.

OPPOSITE BELOW A curving gravel path lined with a bank of bluebells passes under a white-flowered arch of prunus and rhododendron.

LEFT A thatched summer house with rustic pillars stands northeast of the house, fronted by a line of *Stipa calamagrostis*.

BELOW Cornish favourites near the entrance to the garden: azaleas spilling over the path, with *Rhododendron* Smithii Group in the background behind a clump of *R.* 'Azumakagami'.

Glendurgan and Trebah

To bracket together two of the finest gardens in Cornwall – indeed in Britain – would be decidedly cavalier were it not for the fact that they share irresistibly strong geographical, topographical, historical and horticultural genes. For a start they are close neighbours, each occupying 25 acres on the northern shore of the River Helford, less than a mile from the open sea. Both are strung out down deep, sheltered valleys that fall from the level ground on which their unpretentious houses are positioned to little coves some 250 feet/76 metres below. What's more, they were conceived and planted within fifteen years of each other by two brothers, members of one of those prosperous and self-confident mercantile families with which nineteenth-century Cornwall was well endowed.

The Foxes had established their base as shipping agents in Falmouth in the mid-seventeenth century, becoming also early converts to the Quaker faith. In the fulsome portraits of two of the four brothers penned by the *West Briton* newspaper of the time, Alfred was billed as the 'upright, conscientious man of business' and Charles as 'the literary man, with a vast fund of diligently accumulated learning and information'. Like their sibling Robert Were Fox of Penjerrick ('the man of science, with rare store of learning and observation'), they were also passionate gardeners, with the money to indulge their hobby in their holiday homes at Glendurgan and Trebah and easy access to the trans-shipment of the prized exotics being discovered by plant hunters in the far corners of the world.

The two gardens are also remarkably similar in shape and structure – an elongated rectangle that narrows halfway down the hillside as it drops to the water's edge. The configuration of their paths is similar too. A broad horizontal walk passes below the house and its sloping lawn, and then splits into four long and roughly parallel trails following the lines of the valleys and linked by a hatching of subsidiary paths and little bridges across the stream and pools on the valley floor. It's a complicated layout, but growth is so lush here in one of the mildest microclimates in the south-west that the plantings are never in danger of being overburdened by hard landscaping, while the rise and fall of the paths create a feeling of dynamic flow: now you find yourself walking among thickets of bamboos and tree ferns at ground level, now you're almost at canopy level with enormous trees. The views, both longitudinal and latitudinal, are breathtaking.

Alfred Fox bought Glendurgan and its three windswept valleys in 1823 and immediately set about planting shelterbelts,

Views in both gardens have a two-way focus: upwards towards the house, downwards towards the river and the sea.

OPPOSITE Looking across Glendurgan's famous maze, rhododendrons and exotic deciduous and evergreen trees process up to the handsome family house built after a fire in 1837.

LEFT The view reversed: a trio of Chusan palms (*Trachycarpus fortunei*) stands in a small clearing, dwarfed by other trees interleaved into Glendurgan's main valley artery as it drops down to the distant Helford River.

RIGHT At Trebah, the painted bridge arching over the lowest pond seems to reflect the white pillars of the garden room on the late eighteenth-century house built by Charles Fox as a country retreat. A mass planting of hydrangeas colonizes the valley floor before it begins its steep ascent.

including *Pinus radiata*, *P. sylvestris* and other conifers, *Quercus ilex* and other oaks, *Abies alba*, lime, beech and horse chestnut, all underplanted with laurel, salix and other tough shrubs – the range was eclectic, the number huge. A slightly wistful diary entry in 1846 read: 'I . . . cut down many trees to open vistas at my dear Sarah's desire.' Wifely nagging aside, storms, natural deaths and ongoing thinning programmes have always made for a high turnover in the tree population here, but the vigilantly renewed shelterbelts continue to act as a protective cordon, and with an evergreen content of about 60 per cent the overall impression is of permanent, luxuriant vegetation.

Charles Fox came on to the scene at Trebah fifteen years later, in 1838. He too chose pines, holm oaks and beech trees to screen and protect his growing collection of exotics, and like Alfred took advantage of the enthusiasm and expertise of Robert Were Fox to plant many of the rhododendron hybrids being bred with conspicuous success at Penjerrick. The two brothers also planted themselves a camellia walk, and some of the plants survive from the original shipments, together with a

kernel of mighty trees: at Glendurgan copper beeches, a group of *Abies alba*, *Fagus sylvatica* 'Riversii', *Liriodendron tulipifera*, *Taxodium distichum* 'Pendens' and several pine trees; at Trebah five trees now rated champions.

Charles's collection was greatly increased after his death in 1878 by the Asian and American conifers and Chinese bamboos imported by his daughter and son-in-law, Juliet and Edmund Backhouse. Joseph Hooker sought out rhododendrons for the couple, and in one 1880 consignment alone the garden was enriched by the delivery of 300 *Dicksonia antarctica* – Trebah's allotted share of the 3,000 tree ferns distributed among the top ten Cornish gardens of the day (nor did Glendurgan miss out on the spoils). Like many other of the historic Cornish gardens, Trebah has established links with the Royal Botanic Garden, Edinburgh, which has supplied a collection of rare ferns to the area near the cascade.

At Glendurgan, Alfred's son and grandson, George Henry and Cuthbert, continued to maintain the shelterbelts and added many new trees, shrubs and climbers. George was especially

BELOW Only a narrow path separates Mallard Pond and the bottom tip of Trebah from the beach at Polgwidden Cove and the waters of the Helford River.

BELOW The density and complexity of the Trebah plantings, ranging from magnolias and rhododendrons to conifers and pines, cordylines and bamboos, is remarkable.

OPPOSITE Seen from across the valley in the middle of the garden at Glendurgan, an English oak is respectfully surrounded by trees, including *Cupressus macrocarpa* 'Lutea', nothofagus, a Chusan palm and a weeping form of *Cercidiphyllum japonicum*.

interested in conifers and rhododendrons, continuing the family tradition of acquiring many of these from Penjerrick. In keeping with the family's Quaker roots, he planted a then-fashionable Holy Bank with a tree of heaven (*Ailanthus altissima*), a Judas tree (*Cercis siliquastrum*) and a crown of thorns (*Colletia paradoxa*). Trebah has not had the same continuity of family ownership as Glendurgan (which is now, however, in the keeping of the National Trust), but after 1907 it was fortunate to have periods of decline reversed by enlightened incomers – Charles Hawkins Hext and his wife Alice, the racing-car impresario Donald Healey and Major Tony Hibbert, who ensured its survival by creating a dedicated trust in 1990.

It is, however, the Robinsonian fusion of the wild and the ornamental that is particularly effective in the steep-sided woodland setting. In both gardens wave upon wave of specimen trees – conifers like *Cedrus atlantica* Glauca Group, *Cunninghamia lanceolata* and *Cupressus macrocarpa* 'Lutea', *Thuja plicata* and the leaning, narrow-crowned *Taxodium distichum* 'Pendens', broadleaves like the Chilean myrtle (*Luma apiculata*), *Fagus sylvatica* and the unmistakable topknots of the Chusan palm (*Trachycarpus fortunei*) – flanked by scores of rhododendrons, azaleas, magnolias and camellias wash down the hillsides, with clumps of bamboos, ferns and tree ferns bristling beside the stream running along the valley floor.

There is another piece of theatre at Glendurgan: the wildflower meadows that cloak the sides of the three valleys. Early purple orchids, marsh orchids, twayblades and ragged Robin would have colonized the site before Alfred's arrival, and these are now enhanced by spring bulbs and wild flowers including primroses, aquilegias and campions, counted in their thousands.

Trebah has its drifts of bluebells, but in spring the greatest concentration of ground-level colour is to be found in the water garden below the top lawn, where colonies of Candelabra primulas, zantedeschias and skunk cabbages fringe the banks of the watercourse that runs down from a small circular pool into a rill; this then turns into a stream feeding a series of larger and larger pools, culminating in the Mallard Pond just below the wall separating the garden from the beach. In summer the exotics planted in the level ground near the visitor centre – phormiums and agaves, giant echiums and *Strelitzia reginae* – are in flower. Close your eyes and you could be in Tresco.

The famous Glendurgan maze of 1833 on the west side of the valley, based on one in Sydney Gardens in Bath, is a major foliage statement: filaments of low-clipped, glossy cherry laurel (*Prunus laurocerasus*) are squashed close together like squiggles of green toothpaste or a line of leafy bolsters, so that the pattern only emerges clearly when seen from the viewing platform opposite. An echo of this pillowy effect is to be found at Trebah in the densely planted 2-acre strip of *Hydrangea macrophylla* on the western side of the valley. (Trebah also has its maze – not of plants but of paths criss-crossing the valley floor, though its pattern is almost obscured by forests of bamboos, including the galloping *Phyllostachys edulis*.)

Although these two magnificent gardens are recognizably from the same stable, they are very different in atmosphere. This has perhaps something to do with the difference between Alfred 'the man of business' and Charles 'the literary man', perhaps something to do with the stewardship of the two different trusts. Glendurgan feels more consciously ornamental (including the well-mannered Durgan beach, formerly a fishing hamlet, now

OVERLEAF It takes five men to cut the wildflower banks at Glendurgan twice a year, but they are a stunning sight in spring; in the cherry orchard on the valley's eastern flank bluebells surge down the slope beneath a mighty tulip tree and cherry trees in full blossom.

RIGHT *Rhododendron* 'Hinomayo' and *Prunus* 'Shirotae' paired along a sunlit path in the upper part of Badger's Walk on the western side of the valley at Trebah.

OPPOSITE Candelabra primulas (in detail above) have colonized the water garden at Trebah, together with blue-spired *Ajuga reptans*. The stepped rill drops past a rhododendrons and tree ferns through a series of pools ending in a cool and shady fernery.

largely given over to holiday lets), while Trebah is more elemental, retaining a real feeling of plant-huntership.

From the moment of setting foot on Porto Praya, one of the Cape Verde Islands, before making the famous landing in the Galapagos Islands in September 1835, the young Charles Darwin was in a 'chaos of delight': 'Here I first saw the glory of tropical vegetation. Tamarinds, Bananas & Palms were flourishing at my feet . . . It is not only the gracefulness of their forms or the novel richness of their colours, it is the numberless & confusing association that rush together on the mind, & produce the effect.' Looking down the valley plantings of Glendurgan and Trebah in spring can produce something of the same effect.

OPPOSITE, CLOCKWISE FROM TOP LEFT Incidents in the landscapes of these two fine gardens: an entanglement of primroses and bluebells; primroses emerging through the petals of *Magnolia* x *veitchii* 'Peter Veitch'; a stone fox breaking through a camellia at Glendurgan; the large head and glossy leaves of the rare Chatham Island forget-me-not, *Myosotidium hortensia*.

RIGHT Glendurgan's maze, with a rustic thatched summer house at its heart, was planted by Alfred Fox in 1833, drawing on the famous version in the Sydney Gardens at Bath. The improbably glossy swirls of cherry laurel (*Prunus laurocerasus*) are separated by narrow gravel walks and kept trimmed to a height of about 5 feet/1.5 metres.

Barbara Hepworth Sculpture Garden

Barbara Hepworth's love affair with Trewyn Studio and St Ives started with a planning row and ended with a house fire. The little building, shoehorned into one of the narrow cobbled snickets rising above the sandy horseshoe of St Ives Bay and with the parish church as an immediate eye-catcher, stood in the grounds of Trewyn House. In 1949 it was in the council's sights for demolition, along with its garden, but a year of well-orchestrated objections won both buildings a reprieve. At the public auction that followed, Hepworth was the successful bidder for what the sales notice described as 'stonebuilt stone premises and garden (of particular interest to artists and others)'.

Her monumental *Contrapuntal Forms*, destined for the 1951 Festival of Britain, were among the earliest denizens of the garden, followed by a stream of stone and bronze pieces that came and went – or stayed put – over the next quarter of a century. It was a time of which she wrote: 'To have found this spot in Cornwall where nature corresponds so genuinely to my concept of style and my whole feeling has for years been a deep source of joy and satisfaction.' Barbara Hepworth still seems very present at Trewyn. After her death in a fire at the studio in 1975 house and garden became a museum. It somehow survived independently until 1980, when the Tate stepped in.

The 3 acres radiate upwards and outwards from the house, pegged to the cluster of buildings – museum, greenhouse, studio and summer house – that is congregated on the southern edge. Bronze and stone monoliths catch the eye everywhere, and visitors are still actively encouraged to walk through some of them. Hepworth herself always urged her guests to wander round the garden alone: 'Let [the sculptures] look at you,' she urged, 'and they'll speak to you.' The genius of the place is that it is a match for even the largest of the sculptures; it is emphatically not merely a backdrop for the art.

Drawing on the services and inspiration of two friends and neighbours, the composer Priaulx Rainier and the horticulturist Will Arnold-Forster (author of *Shrubs for the Milder Counties*, published in 1948), she grounded and surrounded her pieces with suitably architectural foliage and dramatic or vibrant flowers: agapanthus and hibiscus, brugmansias and euphorbias, *Zantedeschia aethiopica* from South Africa and *Pericallis cruenta* from the Canary Islands, with bougainvillea and plumbago festooning the greenhouse and *Magnolia grandiflora* shading the studio.

The existing trees, which included a copper beech, two large pear trees and several large *Cordyline australis* (the rather rudely named cabbage palm is now so ubiquitous in south-west England that its other common name is the Cornish palm), were joined by *Trachycarpus fortunei*, oak, holly and flowering cherry. Rationalizing the sight lines by acquiring two other small parcels of land from John Milne, the sculptor who had bought Trewyn House, Hepworth planted a now-dominant dawn redwood (*Metasequoia glyptostroboides*), on the topmost boundary, and a fringe of pittosporums and berberis near the greenhouse.

The rose garden which was there when she arrived was swiftly taken apart, and Floribundas, Hybrid Teas and a few species roses are now scattered throughout the site. There are yew and fuchsia hedges, but the most dramatic effect comes from the leafy and exotic specimens planted as a counterpoint to bronze and stone. Palms, yuccas, bamboos and grasses stand tall among climbers and shrubs, making screens or acting as focal points for individual sculptures. Several must have been chosen for the drama of their leaf colour or shape – the spotted laurel, *Aucuba japonica* 'Variegata', for instance, or *Fatsia japonica* with its splayed fingers. The straplike leaves of *Aponogeton distachyos* and their scented white flowers colonize the shallow pond that reflects the narcissus-like outline of *Torso II*.

Although there are plenty of vibrant, largely non-native flowers to catch the eye, the colour scheme is set by the varied grey-greens of trunks and leaves and the grey, white or bronze tints of sculptures, paths and buildings. It is impossible to overemphasize the importance of the weaving together of nature and sculpture by Hepworth's own hands – it is the animus that makes the garden unique. Her guiding principles have been faithfully observed or reinterpreted by a succession of custodians – and, museum crunches permitting, its future is now mercifully secure.

There are some places, like the tiny Norman church at Kilpeck in Herefordshire, Kettle's Yard in Cambridge or Ian Hamilton Finlay's emblematic garden at Little Sparta in Scotland, that display a completely satisfying integrity of vision. Barbara Hepworth's sculpture garden is one of these.

Steps lead up to the conservatory at the top of the garden. Trees and shrubs are thickly planted in this upper part of the garden, and the combination of shade, shadows and foliage makes a fine foil for the twisting growth of *Corymb* (1959).

In spring, euphorbia flowers fill the empty circle of one half of *Two Forms (Divided Circle)*, created in 1969; the other is hung with flowering cherry.

Visible through the eye of the circle is the largest piece in the garden, the two-tier bronze *Four Square (Walk Through)* of 1966.

Visitors can indeed walk through *Four Square (Walk Through)* to view the 1956 *Stone Sculpture (Fugue II)*. Hepworth actively encouraged people to engage physically with her sculptures.

Shining out against its dark green foliage backcloth, the polished bronze *Shaft and Circle* of 1973 stands outside the studio at the foot of the steps leading up to the conservatory.

Trengwainton

Frank Kingdon-Ward, one of the last of the great plant hunters, who had much to do with Trengwainton being put on the horticultural map after 1925, described the ecstasy of coming across a plant unknown in the West: 'The sudden vision is like a physical blow, a blow in the pit of the stomach; one can only gasp and stare. In the face of such unsurpassed loveliness one is afraid to move, as with bated breath one mutters the single word "God!" – a prayer rather than an exclamation.' The National Trust, who took over Trengwainton's 30 acres in 1961, aspires to kindle here the same feelings of astonishment and delight. Trengwainton has trees and shrubs from four continents, some of which flowered in England for the first time in this garden, and subtropical species and cultivars not seen anywhere else in Britain.

Although a house existed on the site in the sixteenth century, the garden is not in the English scheme of things very old: the bones of its distinctive layout were laid out in the nineteenth century and its key plantings in the twentieth. Rose Price, who

BELOW *Dicksonia antarctica* and *Stipa calamagrostis* thrive in the shade of the mature woodland near the entrance to the garden. RIGHT Marsh marigolds (*Caltha palustris*) trail down to the water's edge in the stream garden on the south side of the long drive up to the house.

acquired the estate in 1814 and the Sherriffdom of Cornwall and a baronetcy a year later, was the son of a Jamaican sugar planter. Although by the early eighteenth century the Caribbean island was the wealthiest in the archipelago, sugar had always been a dodgy business. Harvests were perennially threatened by hurricanes and their shipment by battles at sea; more seriously in the long term, prices fell when other markets opened up and new plantations were established elsewhere. But whereas meteorological and commercial fluctuations were a known and largely manageable risk in the sugar trade, the outlawing of slave trafficking in 1807 and of the slave trade itself in 1833 were disasters from which men like Sir Rose were unable to recover. He must have known that the writing was on the wall, when he died in 1834; two years later Trengwainton was sold to pay off his debts.

During the years of prosperity, money was poured into both house and garden. He created a splendid carriage drive to wind from the entrance lodges past an elaborate and revolutionary series of walled and kitchen gardens, designed pleasure grounds with a string of ponds in the valley west of the house, and planted blocks and belts of beech, ash and sycamore to shelter his plantings. In front of the house he laid a wide terrace and sloping lawn to take full advantage of the panoramic views over to St Michael's Mount and the Lizard Peninsula. (Today the drama is slightly marred by a rash of houses in one line of sight, but if you're lucky you may be rewarded by the surreal vision of an enormous naval vessel tethered offshore.)

The surviving trees planted by Sir Rose are now fully mature, but it is the complex of south-facing walled gardens built after 1814 that are his unique legacy. Shaped like an irregular arrowhead, they occupy the lower half of the huge, roughly square kitchen garden with its traditional orchard, glasshouses and chicken, mushroom and bee houses. Their dimensions are supposedly those of Noah's Ark (300 x 50 cubits), a nice conceit. Today they have a slightly mournful, slightly spooky atmosphere that is both powerful and curiously peaceful – at a guess you would date them centuries earlier than the year preceding the Battle of Waterloo, when the Industrial Revolution was already in full swing.

Noah's Ark is divided horizontally into two quite separate strips by tall brick walls and a Cornish hedge (once rather well defined as 'a battered drystone granite wall with vegetation where one might expect coping'), and each is subdivided

which have grown to unusual size. The westernmost one is cool and quiet, given over largely to tender foliage plants, while its neighbour has summer colour from South American plants and a collection of fuchsias, and the largest, central space is themed yellow and white with tender rhododendrons, South African exotics and some fine magnolias. The two compartments on the eastern side are the most atmospheric, dominated by majestic magnolias: *M.* x *veitchiii* 'Peter Veitch' is partnered by plants from the Canary Island and South Africa, *M. campbellii* with others from New Zealand and Australia.

Bolitho did not concentrate his energies on this small but vital area alone. He planted 10 further acres of woodland and opened up the long, previously culverted stream that runs between the two parallel driveways leading up to the house, fringing its verges with Candelabra primulas, skunk cabbages, crocosmias, astilbes and zantedeschias and other spring- and summer-flowering marginals, with tree ferns and *Rhododendron johnstoneanum* and *R. tephropeplum*.

Price was responsible for laying the original drive, the Long Walk, but Bolitho opened up glades off it to reveal dense plantations of rhododendrons, camellias and hydrangeas planted beneath the canopy of beech and other native trees. To stock these he enlisted the help of three of the finest plantsmen of this or any age – his cousins J.C. Williams of Caerhays and P.D. Williams of Lanarth, and Canon Boscawen of Ludgvan – and their gifts helped swell the flood of rare and completely unknown seeds that poured in after Kingdon-Ward's 1927–8 expedition to Assam and Burma, to which Bolitho was a subscriber. He was fortunate that his head gardener of thirty years' standing, Alfred Creek (there were only three gardeners in a hundred years), was a master of the propagating art, and Trengwainton became a byword for species and hybrid rhododendrons in the horticultural show world. Many – *maccabeanum*, *elliottii*, *taggianum* and *cinnabarinum* subsp. *xanthocodon* Concatenans Group – flowered in the UK for the first time here. Second only to these are the collections of camellias, magnolias, species and Lacecap hydrangeas, michelias, banksias and acacias.

Since acquiring the garden in 1961 the National Trust, together with Simon Bolitho (his family continues to live in the house), has revived the plantings, rationalized the design and created new areas south of the walled gardens, and the rejuvenation of the estate owes much to their partnership. But it was the joint vision of Price and Bolitho that has made Trengwainton a treasure-house of plants in two very different settings: a forcing ground for tender rarities, and the re-creation of a distant landscape within an English woodland setting. Just one regret: how much more fun it would be to set off down those two elongated drives not on foot but astride a horse or bowling along in an open carriage.

TOP The estate, approached from a small road up a hillside in zigzag sweeps, has panoramic views stretching from the ha-ha in front of the house across park and farmland over Mount's Bay to the Lizard.
ABOVE Looking down from one of the raised beds in the kitchen garden, tilted towards the sun.

internally. In the topmost strip, a kitchen garden with a charming head gardener's cottage set into the main wall overlooks a long and narrow rectangle divided into five. So as to give early vegetables, fruit and flowers required for the household the best chance of survival, an ingenious mind devised beds in the central and southern enclosures that slope upwards to the top of the low dividing walls, orientating them towards the west to minimize frost damage.

The tip of the 'arrowhead', the southern section, consists of a further five irregularly shaped compartments, and it is here that Trengwainton's other key player joins with Price. Lieutenant Colonel (later Sir) Edward Bolitho, member of a prominent Cornish family who acquired the estate in 1867, was a collector of rare and unusual trees and shrubs – one contemporary recalls that he admitted to gardening only 'above the knee', ignoring low-growing beauties. He commandeered Price's five warm and sheltered enclosures to house prize specimens, some of

LEFT FROM TOP Candelabra primulas jostle with astilbes and other moisture-lovers in the colourful stream garden; signs of activity in the head gardener's bothy; *Rhododendron facetum*. *R. yunnanense*, *R.* 'Loder's White' and *R. arboreum* line the entrance drive.

ABOVE FROM TOP *Camellia* x *williamsii* 'J.C. Williams', its flowers pale pink with a golden heart, are to be found throughout the garden, while a pure white astilbe (cultivar name unknown) is planted in the stream garden.

Chygurno

In 1913 the Post-Impressionist artist Laura Knight painted a relaxed family portrait of a bearded man in plus-fours, his pipe clamped to his mouth and his young daughter to his hip; her elder sister sits swinging her legs on a tree trunk in front of a woodland cascade. The setting is the beautiful Lamorna Valley which, unusually in the far west of Cornwall, runs down a heavily wooded valley on its way to the sea. The sitter, Knight's friend and fellow painter Samuel John Birch, had been nicknamed Lamorna to distinguish him from a painter of the same surname and also because of his love for the place, which was a favourite haunt of the Newlyn School of painters during the years before the Great War.

High above the narrow lane leading to the harbour – and as far removed in spirit from *Lamorna Birch and His Two Daughters* as it is possible to imagine – there perches a remarkable small garden. The house gazes straight out to sea past a twisted and twin-trunked Scots pine that is the guardian of the place. The sturdy stone house was built in 1908 by two politically active women who offered it as a refuge to fellow suffragettes recently released from prison; when Robert and Carol Moule came upon it in 1997 it had lain unoccupied for over twenty years and the garden was wildly overgrown.

Hacking through the undergrowth, pickaxeing the granite outcrops that form the bedrock of the garden and shouldering boulders out of the way of naturally dictated routes across and down the steep slope that makes up most of the 4-acre garden took the Moules five years. Giant steps were carved from slabs of granite or sweet chestnut and paths from granite chippings: they bought hundreds of 20-foot-long 6-inch pipes, taped them together and shot 80 tons of the stuff down from the top of the garden to the bottom.

The house surround, tamed by decking and a stone terrace, is a sheltered spot with a rockery where aeoniums, aloes and other succulents thrive (although to avoid a repetition of a wipe-out of the treasured aeoniums suffered during the severe winter of 2007, the specimens most at risk are now moved each year to the protection of a fleece-lined greenhouse). From the house a broad pathway acts as a central runway between plantings of palms and exotics and where the path disappears from view the land starts its freefall to the road 262 feet/80 metres below. A spaghetti network of paths runs between the thickets of planting sprouting among the rocky outcrops.

LEFT ABOVE Approaching Chygurno from an upper road, the hawthorn tree and clumps of senecio and hebe reveal the slate roof of the sturdy 1908 house and a glimpse of the distant sea but give no idea of the exciting garden laid out behind and below.

LEFT BELOW The finely carved nameplate is surrounded by a cloud of Mexican daisies, *Erigeron karvinskianus*.

RIGHT A solitary Monterey pine stands sentinel behind a mound of purple-flowered *Rhododendron* 'Fastuosum Flore Pleno' at the highest point in the garden, introducing the superb view over Lamorna Cove and the path zigzagging down to the bottom of the slope.

Every inch of path – passing here among ferns and tree ferns – had to be hacked through granite bedrock on the steep slope before being laid to gravel or wooden walkway.
OPPOSITE The garden is essentially linear, with a global mix of plants grouped with both artistry and a sense of discipline.

Collections of rhododendrons, hydrangeas, camellias and magnolias are interspersed with exotics and grasses; stands of bamboos create a dark tunnel; and seen from the woodland area at the bottom of the garden a collection of tree ferns makes more of an impact than they would in a larger space. Groups of agapanthus, commelina and celmisia sparkle blue, crocosmias add touches of orange, and everywhere you look flowers and

foliage catch the eye – flapping banana plants, architectural leucadendrons and spectacular puyas, the distinctive Mohican-fringe flowers of *Grevillea* 'Bronze Rambler' and *G. barklyana*, fluffy-flowered acacias and tender metrosideros, Canary Island foxgloves and Chatham Island forget-me-nots.

If I were planning to create a garden in a coastal crow's nest, my research would begin (and probably end) at Chygurno.

Tremenheere

Tremenheere must be one of the most exciting contemporary gardens to be created on a large scale in Cornwall since the Eden Project (which is of course not a garden at all). Visiting in 2009, it was possible to admire the concept, the way an ancient wooded valley had ingested new plantings and sculptures, and to look forward to the completion of sculptural works celebrating earth and sky. The place was, however, in its infancy then, and difficult for someone without its originator's breadth of vision to envisage entire.

Given the galloping generative power of the Cornish climate, what a difference a couple of years makes! The wooded valley across the bridge on the south-west perimeter is now a primeval forest, its canopy of tall native beech, ash and chestnut trees sheltering an army of tree ferns and groves of unfamiliar bamboos including the immaculately upright *Chusquea gigantea,* and the blue-fading-to-bruise-coloured *Himalayacalamus hookerianus.* The bole of a fallen mammoth – a beech tree that has lain decomposing for three decades – is host to a small colony of ferns, and as you climb up the wooden boardwalk leading over the oozy valley floor you pass by subtropical plants, native shrubs and half-hardy

RIGHT From the oak wood at the top of the garden, the view pans round from the buildings of Penzance through St Michael's Mount to the ancient woodland at the bottom of the valley. The central grass strip has collections of subtropical plants; the roof on the right belongs to a *camera obscura.*
BELOW A narrow raised boardwalk leading over a green-encrusted pond in the lower woodland creates a jungle-like atmosphere amid lichened trees and native and tree ferns.

ABOVE LEFT The boardwalk winds along the stream through woodland plantings in the valley garden, passing pools and giant fallen trees in a primeval landscape.

ABOVE RIGHT Emerging from the shadows into the light and mounting the steps to the raised gazebo at the top of the valley, you encounter *Dasylirion longisssimum*, *Yucca linearifolia*, *Ischyrolepis subverticillata* and *Pennisetum alopecuroides.*

rhododendrons woven among them. A little stream runs through, feeding small ponds surrounded by ferns and bog plants; the two more recently excavated near the bridge will in time also become absorbed into their woodland setting.

This deep valley occupies just one tranche of Tremenheere's 11 acres. Glimpsed through the trees is the mezzanine storey of land: a broad, grassy band which had been farmed since the 1820s for strawberries and vegetables. When Neil Armstrong arrived in 1997 there were still residual crops to be found among the undergrowth. This sun-bleached area now has a more exotic harvest from New Zealand, South Africa and South America: banksias, bananas, beschornerias, echiums, aloes, cacti and phormiums complemented by perennials such as *Euphorbia stygiana*, *Kniphofia thomsonii* and watsonias with their ravishing wild-gladiolus flowers. *Butia capitata* makes a strong, stubby avenue, and monkey puzzles and substantial clumps of restios and grasses help fix the plantings into the

edge of the slope furthest from Mount Bay. Some are set in gravel, which not only aids drainage and heat retention but also gives a more ornamental character to this important mezzanine part of the garden.

On the brow of the hill a hanging bluebell wood of Turkey oaks curves round towards the lower woodland valley; the stunning distant view of Mount Bay and St Michael's Mount is caught between the two. In the grassy middle band, at the junction of the two, is a little quarry and an olive grove, and a path leads back into woodland where two ponds are surrounded by tree ferns and an eye-catching white splash of *Zantedeschia aethiopica*.

In the Cornish dialect Tremenheere means 'standing stone found', and although only half a dozen artworks have found a home here, their substantial presence fulfils Neil Armstrong's stated aim to create 'moments of wonder'. Made of wood or stone, they're positioned to harmonize with their surroundings, whether open hillside or deep woodland. In the low-lying valley the irregularly scored trunks of eleven trees, the work of the Japanese artist Kishio Suga, symbolize man's journey through life. At the upper level the same artist's disturbing piece has scaffolding poles rammed into bamboos (representing the rigidity of Japanese society) and then trapped within cages (representing repressed energy). David Mach's tall oak stumps – menhirs to a generation brought up on Asterix – charred and shaped and oiled, are like a family struck by lightning, standing motionless in a circular dip in the oak wood, surrounded by ferns, natural vegetation and tall trees.

There are three other installations which are reliant on the effects of natural and artificial light. The largest of these, a round granite-clad stone pillbox placed at the end of the succulent/desert planting and answering the bulk of St Michael's Mount on the horizon, is James Turrell's *Skyspace*. Enthusiasts for the American artist's work will have followed the development of his celestial observatories on both sides of the Atlantic: *Roden Crater* in Arizona, *Ganzfeld* in Germany and a *Skyspace* on stilts at Houghton Hall in Norfolk. Seen from the air, his domed elliptical roof at Tremenheere looks like an all-seeing eye – shades of Mordor – but from inside, where LED lights focus up the whitewashed wall behind a sloping wooden bench, the captive audience's attention is drawn irresistibly to the changing clouds and light in the sky seen through the oval glass panel set into the roof.

Also Turrell's work is an underground tank called *Agua Oscura*. As you plunge from the dappled sunlight of a streamside path in the lower woodland into a pitch-black corridor, the senses are alerted to discomfort, possibly danger, before they become accustomed to the unfamiliar darkness and make out the shadows and flickers of light on the end wall. It is the only one of his works to make use of exclusively natural light, and as with Suga's work it is a disconcerting experience. By contrast, local artist Billy Wynter's *Camera Obscura* is a contemporary version of the image-projecting device used by nineteenth-century artists and botanists to help them make accurate representations of living plants; it has something of the rarified interest of the cabinets of curiosities of the period that crop up in letters home written by gilded youths on the Grand Tour (Seymour Tremenheere was one such European traveller, travelling rather foppishly in a distinctive yellow carriage).

Cornwall as a whole has embraced the subtropical opportunities offered by climate change, and most gardens of note now have their share of exotic plantings. At Tremenheere, however, the rhythmical contours of the land within the garden and the dramatic scenery beyond it balance out the boldness of the plantings so that they never seem alien in the landscape. The garden, although surrounded by agricultural land, with road noise bringing a constant reminder that Penzance and its port and heliport are just a few miles away, seems very remote – the sparrowhawks hovering regularly at eye level beside *Skyspace* certainly seem to think so.

BELOW David Mach's gathering of blackened oak shapes (are they friend or foe?) stands among wild flowers in a clearing made in the oak and bluebell wood at the top of the slope.

BOTTOM The all-seeing eye of James Turrell's *Skyspace* zeroes in on the changing weather patterns above the garden.

Trewidden

The Bolithos of Trewidden arrived in Penzance in about 1789, more than a century after the Foxes of Glendurgan and Trebah had made a similar journey, establishing themselves as a local force in Falmouth. The two families were headed by men of the same kidney: tough and astute businessmen, spreading their nets wide and adept at grasping new opportunities. Among the pies in which the Bolithos had fingers were tanning (the trade originally followed by Thomas, the patriarch of the clan) pilchard-seining, tin-smelting, banking and politics. Appropriately, the 1830s house built by Thomas's grandson stands on the site of an ancient opencast tin mine, and the family's industrial roots remain evident in the garden today.

The Bolithos' interest in horticulture passed down the generations in the same way as happened with the Trengwainton branch of the same family and with the Williams of Caerhays. Indeed, the three families became closely linked: Mary, daughter of Thomas Bedford Bolitho (1835–1915), married Charles Williams, but moved back to Trewidden on his death in 1955. When she died the estate went to her cousin Alverne, the son of Simon Bolitho of Trengwainton.

Like Tremenheere Sculpture Garden a few miles away, the garden is very near Penzance and within sight of St Michael's Mount. Trewidden, however, is set in a bowl of land, and this lack of a coastal focus, together with the long and winding entrance drive (even though it is flanked by palm trees and camellias rather than an avenue of native trees), makes it feel initially more traditionally English than its neighbour. Inside the garden proper, though, the Cornish character reasserts itself, for in the second half of the nineteenth century Edward Bolitho protected the exposed perimeter to the north and south and especially to the west with shelterbelt trees, so as to create a suitable environment for a range of Asian and southern-hemisphere introductions; these woodland plantings were laced together with a network of winding paths.

His son Thomas Bedford gave the garden a new sense of direction when he obtained a quantity of *Dicksonia antarctica*, the tree ferns being disseminated in many of the top Cornish gardens by Treseder Nursery in Truro at the end of the nineteenth century. T.B.'s daughter Mary moved the garden on again: starting in 1897 with *Magnolia obovata,* which is now one of Trewidden's champion trees, she was responsible for augmenting and rejuvenating the garden from 1955 until her death twenty years later.

LEFT ABOVE *Camellia* x *williamsii* 'Grand Jury'.
LEFT BELOW *Magnolia* x *veitchii* 'Peter Veitch'.

RIGHT Along the curving drive, a metasequoia has established itself with a line of camellias in a Cornish hedge. This ancient feature, unique to the county, is neither a true hedgerow nor a wall, but a stone-faced earth hedge-bank with shrubs or trees growing along the top.

BELOW LEFT The trunk of this
champion dawn redwood,
Metasequoia glyptostroboides,
was among the first to be
planted in Britain and is one of
the largest in the country.
BELOW RIGHT *Aponogeton
distachyos*, the water hawthorn,
spreading in a rusty bowl in the
walled garden (top).
Fallen petals surround a
magnificent *Magnolia* x *veitchii*
'Peter Veitch', the largest
specimen in Britain (bottom).

In essence, Trewidden is a plant-hunters' trophy garden – but its 15 acres/6 hectares conceal a number of surprises. In shape it would be more or less square, were it not for two irregularities: the Western Plantation and the adjoining Camellia Garden, which form a triangle on the south-western perimeter (protected on its two most vulnerable sides by windbreak trees); and another outlying chunk, the self-contained South Garden, which lies off the entrance drive next to the car park. The Camellia Garden was planted by Mary Williams. Formerly set out in stock beds, many of the 300-strong collection now huddle together in an informal agglomeration along paths and in glades.

The surprises come as you work your way clockwise from the explosion of camellias through the different parts of the garden. There are individual eye-catchers, including a Cornish hedge (actually a free-standing wall that's basically a stone sandwich with a soil filling) dramatically planted with laurels, bamboos and camellias. A stand of bamboo near the bridge that leads into T.B.'s tree fern dell has been worked into a great bending curtain. Ancient trees rear up along the route: a solitary and rather hideous South American jelly palm (*Butia capitata*); a native of southern Japan, *Castanopsis cuspidata*, towering over an old red telephone box; a mighty *Magnolia* 'Trewidden Belle' in the walled garden (once part of the kitchen garden and now being revitalized with a butterfly border); and, a final champion flourish near the exit, a mightily gnarled old dawn redwood (*Metasequoia glyptostroboides*).

Many of the woodland areas are cool and quiet and secret in feeling, and also somewhat strange. The heart of the garden is occupied by a collection of tree ferns that have colonized a

pit once occupied by the workings of the tin mine – a surreal but perfect place for them to settle their bulky, belligerent bodies – the sides of which are shored up by resuscitated lengths of railway track. The adjoining Burrows are likewise pits gouged out of the soil; angular pieces of mining debris still project from beds and paths, but a rockery and pool now occupy the largest hole. Near by is a newer form of crater, created when bombs were discharged on the garden during the Second World War.

Further west comes a more contemporary surprise: a life-size whale tail sinking back into a woodland pond. The drama of anatomy in water – waving, drowning and everything in between – has long been a potent symbol. Think only of Tennyson's evocation of King Arthur's 'great brand Excalibur' being flourished above the lake near the killing field of Lyonesse; or

Giles Kent's threatening series of spiked wooden fists thrusting out of the stream that flows into the lake at Burghley House in Lincolnshire. Trewidden's whale used to play the kind of watery tricks beloved of Elizabethan garden-makers, like Chatsworth's copper (and literally weeping) willow, by rocking and spouting; now it is motionless, spent but still a force guarding the Japanese lantern on the little central island.

For the beauty of its setting and the interest of its plant collection, Trewidden cannot be ranked among the most spectacular Cornish gardens. But the plant-hunting legacy and the industrial legacy go hand-in-hand here in a most immediate and forceful way. That is what makes it stand out from all the rest.

BELOW The whale tail rising from the pond, ringed by daffodils and gunneras, was a christening present to the present owner's son.

Trevarno

On my first visit to Trevarno I drove there not by the recommended route but through a maze of one-track lanes with grudging passing places, hemmed in by banks of wild flowers which gave me a clear image of the estate's setting – magical but surprisingly lonely – during its nineteenth-century heyday. When I finally reached the wooded valley, I was almost expecting to find a briar patch with rusting gates clanged shut rather than a vibrant and bustling enterprise and gardens almost fully restored.

Since 1996 a major restoration project has been under way at Trevarno, and comparisons will inevitably be drawn with the once-lost gardens of Heligan. There are differences in style and presentation between the two – in the tricky balance between the historically purist and the acceptably entertaining Trevarno does tilt (especially in its literature) towards the latter. More noticeable, however, is the impression that this too is an estate brought back from the brink of decay with genuine passion and commitment. In Trevarno's case, all 750 acres of it. To see and understand both the challenge and the incentive, ignore the prescribed route and make first for the walled enclosure at the very heart of the 70 acre gardens. Alongside a shattered glasshouse that once sheltered peaches and vines are overgrown arbours and cross-arbours encouraging cool perambulation, while raised beds have been resurrected among the surrounding disorder into neat and productive rows.

The spacious, peacock-embellished lawn adjoining the attractive, cream-painted villa and its splendid conservatory is effectively an antechamber, empty save for a generous border spilling over with a bold mix of cannas, hebes, yuccas, tree ferns, hydrangeas and a bright red azalea. Beyond, glimpsed through the branches of a pair of giant cedars, portico columns are the backdrop to the so-called Italian Garden, actually a successful marriage of roses and camellias – an outer hedge of *C.* x *williamsii* 'Jury's Yellow' fronted by a lower hedge of 'Cornish Spring', with individual pillars of *C.* x *w.* 'Donation' for added drama.

These two areas might be expected to set the scene for the exuberant and colourful gardens laid out on the slope below, but they are both modern and quite different in mood

The 70 acres of garden represent a gentleman's estate of ambition and imagination. Even the potting shed is Gothick, the focus of a striking planting of copper-coloured *Acer palmatum* var. *dissectum* 'Atropurpureum' and a single Chusan palm, *Trachycarpus fortunei*.

BELOW Peacocks have established a noisy, preening presence on the lawn adjoining the house, flanked by an avenue of flowering cherries.

RIGHT A wrought-iron gate leads into the serpentine garden created in 1790. It lies between the yew tunnel and the north wall of the upper walled garden.

from the rest. A clue is given, however, by the little cottage perched on rising ground above the house lawn, for Trevarno contains a host of ornamental garden buildings, ranging from a dovecote to an icehouse, a gazebo to a rotunda, a white Edwardian summerhouse to a decorative potting shed clamped to a wall; best of all is the most sumptuous Gothick boathouse imaginable, reflected in the waters of a long and rectangular lake. Although the existence of an estate here can be traced back to 1245, it was a much later succession of families who were largely responsible for planting magnificent trees, and for shaping the gardens, and filling them with little buildings from which to view them. Here are the nineteenth and early twentieth centuries at play, and highly enjoyable it is to observe the place through their eyes.

The several separate gardens were laid out to be reached individually on foot or by carriage, and are knitted together by an abundance of paths and steps. An ancient yew tunnel has been preserved at the top of the slope, but the central tranche between the house lawn and the lake is occupied by a gracious arrangement of lawns studded with specimen trees and shrubs (including an eye-catching pattern of low-growing claret-coloured acers), with a trio of Picturesque features grouped at the short, eastern end of the lake above a formal cascade: a savage-looking rockery, a rockwork grotto and a stone version of King Arthur's round table. The nearby pinetum is made infinitely more attractive than many of its kind by the happy combination of rising ground, fine views, a tall tree canopy and a naturalistic underplanting of foxgloves and ferns. The lake is *sui generis* too, for in addition to that marvellous boathouse it has two islands, one crowned by gunnera, the other by a swamp cypress.

The western half of the gardens, below the Italian Garden, is the entrance drive, where carriages rolled to the house through a beautiful wooded valley, misty in spring with bluebells. Streams run through the lower part of the valley, providing the opportunity for a bamboo plantation and a bog garden. Above all these, but by no means obtruding themselves on the landscape, are a herd of reindeer and a National Collection of daffodils reputed to

BELOW The Italian Garden is ravishing in spring when the pink flowers start to spangle the camellias, clipped to form V-shaped edging and sculpted pillars. The beds in between are filled with roses, and a classical 'ruin' in the background gives a hint of Rome.

flower from late December through to early May. The children's adventure playground is likewise hidden in the woods, while the National Museum of Gardening's purpose-built shed is tucked away by the car park.

The inward-looking gardens are set within an outward-looking estate, and a walk has been devised through open country and farmland, taking in a diverse collection of landmarks: Sithney Church, RNAS Culdrose, Goonhilly Earth Station and Halzephron Cliff. There is even a view of the sea near Porthleven. It rounds off a visit to an enterprising, well-conceived and finely executed work of garden restoration. All power to the elbows of Mike Sagin and Nigel Helsby, engineers of this remarkable regeneration.

OPPOSITE LEFT ABOVE
A Picturesque rockery, a suitably gloomy grotto and a re-creation of King Arthur's round table are congregated at the far end of the lake, behind the shallow cascade.

OPPOSITE LEFT BELOW The large and sophisticated boathouse, complete with slate roof, scalloped bargeboards and pointed turret, was designed by Percy Bickford-Smith, son of a nineteenth-century owner who was responsible for many of the garden's striking features.

OPPOSITE RIGHT ABOVE A group of beech trees planted in the late eighteenth century as part of a tree-planting programme designed to conceal the deposits of mining waste from the big house.

OPPOSITE RIGHT BELOW The sloping woodland valley on the perimeter of the garden is planted principally with beech, enabling bluebells to flower in their thousands in April and May.

BELOW There are some 2,600 different varieties of daffodil planted in a dedicated field without the curtilage of the garden, overlooked by Monterey pines. Their flowering season can stretch from late December to May.

St Michael's Mount

St Michael's Mount was apparently formed as a result of a clash of the Earth's tectonic plates 275 million years ago – or thereabouts. The granite pyramid is a landmark from the Lizard to Land's End and acts as a borrowed sculpture to Trevarno, Trengwainton, Trewidden, Tremenheere and many other gardens positioned for safety and scenic reasons on the high ground above Mount's Bay. Lying at a 45-degree angle to the south-west, off the Normandy coast at Avranches, is Mont-Saint-Michel. In a few basic respects they are mirror images: roughly equal in height, square mileage and population. Both have gardens set within the inner curve of their respective bays, giving them a modicum of protection from the gales and sea spray that ravage their exposed coastlines.

The historical connection between the two is more superficial and fleeting. In about 1080 the English island and onshore holdings – and its revenues – were ceded to the monastery of Mont-St-Michel as a reward for support for William the Conqueror as he launched his English campaign. And in 1135 it was Mont-St-Michel's abbot, Bernard du Bec, an enthusiastic builder, who commissioned a new priory for this part of his English fiefdom. (Curiously, it seems that some 750 years later, in 1828, the boot might have been on the other foot: Sir John St Aubyn toyed with the idea of buying Mont-St-Michel after the defeat of Napoleon – Admiral Charles Fielding commented on hearing the story that 'it would have been curious to be the possessor of both . . . he would have had some difficulty in tunnelling a road from one to the other.')

After 1144 the island was owned for nearly four centuries by Church or Crown and for just over three and a half by a surprisingly small number of private families – Elizabeth I's adviser Robert Cecil, the Bassetts of Tehidy and, from 1599 to 1954, twelve generations of St Aubyns (created Lords St Levan in 1887). The 3rd Baron gave the island to the National Trust in 1954 but negotiated a 999-year lease to secure for the family the right to live in the castle and manage its enterprises.

The small rocky outcrop 400 yards/366 metres from mainland Britain but accessible to it for just a few hours a day is fascinating not only for the comfortable fusion of eight centuries of architectural history, but also for the diversity of its setting. Given that the castle sits on a windswept piece of granite with absolutely no protection from the ravaging easterlies, where extremely wild and wet winters are followed inexorably by extremely hot and dry summers, a token garden might have seemed more than adequate. The harsh winter of 2007 saw 50 per cent of the tender plants that appreciate the mild Gulf Stream temperatures wiped out; worst off were the succulents for which the garden is renowned, including a prized collection of aeoniums. Two years later the same thing happened again.

Lesser gardeners would be demoralized, but they're an inventive and resilient lot at the Mount, where an abseiling course is a prerequisite to securing an outside job. A combination of a 20-foot/6-metre sea wall and shelter plantings of bullet-proof vegetation helps push the prevailing south-westerly winds up and over.

For several decades past, as advised by Helen Dorrien-Smith, the planting policy was geared towards making the most of the Mount's arid environment and pushing out the boundaries of what it was possible to grow outside rather than under glass. Now, under Michael Harvey, an American designer with a long Cornish association, an ambitious ten-year master plan is being pursued which aims to increase the number of flowering plants and spread the interest and colour over a longer period, to introduce new drought-tolerant subshrubs and hardy succulents and, in order to give different areas a stronger sense of place, to concentrate species more coherently (but still loosely) according to climate zones. It's a path that many contemporary gardeners and garden designers are following, but here, where the available planting space is restricted to strips and pockets competing with dramatic slabs of rock, it seems particularly appropriate.

The scattering of cottages adjoining the harbour – where the flotilla of small boats arrives to relay visitors across the narrow strip of water – is separated from the castle perched at the apex by a broad band of oaks, sycamores and other native trees. A cobbled way leads up to the eighteenth-century battery and the castle gate, between trees, shrubs and herbaceous perennials familiar around the country. The southern-hemisphere plantings are to be found on the climbing wall on the seaward side.

Before the paths and terraces start their steep ascent to the castle, a semi-informal avenue of phormiums and cordylines at sea level, with stands of *Puya chilensis* for added impact, is an unusual first line of defence against the

Lying 400 yards/366 metres from the Cornish coast but accessible by foot a few hours a day, the almost perfectly conical island with a fairytale castle at its apex is being planted with a new sense of purpose.

RIGHT The garden rises on terraces beneath the castle wall, lined by the distinctive heads of cordyline and trachycarpus, a single giant *Echium candicans* and a vibrant cerise mat of daisy-flowered lampranthus. On the right a Mexican *Furcraea* is identified by its yucca-like leaves, although its triffid-sized flower spike is not visible.

elements; these, together with a sloping wildflower meadow awash in May with bluebells and campions, and a Second World War pillbox, add up to an unusual scene-setter. As you round the curve, you suddenly observe the famous view of the castle anchored into the rockface, and from then on the journey is essentially a rugged and vertical one. The charm of delicately hanging flowers like fuchsias tends to be lost, and it is the individual show-stealers such as aloes and agaves or blockbusters like the ice plants sheeting the castle wall that set the parameters.

The first stage of the climb up narrow grass paths and steep, often alternately stepped, stone steps has the Mediterranean as its theme; a few of the aeoniums surviving from the last massacre were replanted opposite the original bed and interspersed with santolinas and salvias, cistus and lavenders. The second level is held together by a repeat-planting of rosemary (elsewhere lithodora and *Aloe polyphylla* take over as rhythm-makers). Then comes a small, dry triangle given over to succulents – echeverias and the like, with a large agave as a plump centrepiece – which will eventually work themselves into the horticultural equivalent of a coral reef.

Looking from the opposite end of the telescope, over the south wall of the castle, there's a sheer 200-foot/61-metre drop down to a trio of long and narrow formal walled gardens, designed in the late eighteenth century to be seen from above and now reinvented by Michael Harvey. Arranged by colour, the long and narrow beds are surrounded by a glazed, barley-twist pebble edging; underfoot is stone paving, some of it patterned, and mellow old bricks. The flowers in the first enclosure tend towards the pastel: the highight is the very rare

BELOW LEFT A stolid stone staircase, stepped in parts – allegedly to prevent ladies from showing too much ankle – rises steeply to the castle; at the top the wall is hung with a curtain of purple ice plants.
BELOW RIGHT As the path ascends to the top of the slope, eyes turn from the plants clinging to its sides towards the compelling views out to sea.

LEFT On their upwards journey, visitors come unawares upon the Coral Bed, a small-scale rockery planted with sempervivums, echeverias and aeoniums in a ravishing palette of purple, turquoise and pale green.

ABOVE The craggy and fissured rockface at the top of the Mount merges seamlessly into the rearing bulk of the castle; its known history stretches back to the twelfth century.

Pericallis lanata, paired with *Tulbaghia violacea* 'Silver Lace'. The lower, slightly sloping second level has a warmer tone characterized by hardy lemons combined with Balearic Island hyericums and *Libertia* 'Goldfinger'; and the lowest has hotter colours still, with a coral tree, *Erythrina crista-galli*, trained against the wall and subtropical fuchsias planted with trailing grevilleas and terrestrial orchids.

This ornamental trio lies between two terraces created in the Victorian period. While in summer the walled gardens have a stifling microclimate, the August temperature among the proteas and leucadendrons in the hot bed on the west terrace has been known to reach 138°F/59°C, and the terraces themselves create a storage-heater effect – the granite is never cold to the touch. The rock face is more dominant here, colonized by other succulents from South Africa.

As the Mount's new plantings mature, it will be fascinating to see whether they live up to their change of direction and develop into an exceptional garden. Until then, the power of the rock face and the impossibly romantic profile of the castle are enough to be going on with. During the 1930s, the St Aubyns' butler whiled away his leisure time fashioning a model of the castle from champagne corks. It was the perfect medium in which to reproduce the fabric of the building, and expresses too the island's combination of resilience and impermanence.

ABOVE Steep indeed is the drop from the castle to the boulder-strewn shoreline. Below the path three walled gardens created in three narrow strips in the 1780s are being revitalized with new planting; and on the right is the close-mown enclosure of the Tortoise Lawn.

LEFT Although the Long Walk is the central spine of the garden, the Middle Terrace is its heart. Cross-paths lead off from the long path lined with *Phoenix* palms and *Cordyline australis* into geometrical spaces of different features and plantings. *Agave salmiana* var. *ferox* leans aggressively over the path.

OPPOSITE A flight of weathered granite steps at right angles to the Middle Terrace terminates in an 1841 figurehead of Neptune, rescued from a wrecked ship. The terracotta pots were designed by the first Lord Proprietor, Augustus Smith, who acquired the Isles of Scilly on a 99-year-lease in 1834.

OVERLEAF Tresco is part of the archipelago of five islands lying off the tip of Cornwall, and the garden faces St Mary's and Samson on its south and south-western sides. Hewn from a cliff cut into granite bedrock, it is a haven for exotics and succulents from all over the world. Shelterbelt trees and a high holm oak hedge screen the ruin of the old abbey, and dotted among the trees, shrubs and flowers are specimens of *Cordyline australis*, *Phoenix canariensis* and *Jubaea chilensis*, palms that dominate the garden grid at every turn.

Tresco

Nowhere in Britain will you find a better-orchestrated display of plants from Australia, New Zealand, South Africa and other faraway countries than at Tresco, in the group of islands that has cartwheeled itself off from mainland Britain into the Atlantic Ocean 30 miles south-west of Land's End. All over the garden they shoulder aside (and are occasionally shouldered aside by) more familiar and less flamboyant plants the pelargoniums and ceanothus, hebes and honeysuckles familiar to borders the rest of the UK over. The helicopter ride ito Tresco s expensive and the boat may with very good reason be referred to by locals as the *Sickonian*, but it's worth multiple inconveniences to reach this fantastic place, where echiums and aeoniums are weeds, pelargoniums are trimmed by lawnmower, and agapanthus grow in their hundreds of thousands not only in the garden but also among the neighbouring sand dunes.

There was a monastic settlement on Tresco in the eleventh century, but the island is now indissolubly linked with a single family. In 1834 Augustus Smith leased the Isles of Scilly from the Duchy of Cornwall, and the five generations who succeeded him as Lord Proprietor have managed the tall order of filling his giant gardening boots. One of the most exciting things about Tresco is the feeling that plant-hunting is not only alive and well but it is still an essential pastime for the country gentry: Robert Dorrien-Smith, who took over the running in the early 1970s and has overseen the gathering of plants for the new Mediterranean garden, is following in the tradition established by his forebears in more leisurely but more challenging times. For those men the euphoria of observing plants growing in the wild in Western Australia, New Zealand, the Canary Islands and South Africa, and of seeing them flourish when transported and transplanted back home, must have been precisely that experienced by Joseph Paxton when the giant *Victoria amazonica* waterlily for which he'd built a dedicated tank at Chatsworth produced its first enormous bloom.

The main body of the garden laid out by Augustus Smith between 1834 and 1858 is defined structurally by three broad gravel paths – the Long Walk and the Middle and Top Terraces – which stretch westwards from the house. The fourth main artery, by contrast, bisects the garden from north to south, running from the Top Terrace straight down a dramatic stone staircase, marked as it passes through the Middle Terrace (the heart of the garden) by towering Canary Island palms; the topmost flight is crowned by and derives its name from a mammoth figurehead from a sunken ship that represents Neptune, god of the sea.

BELOW The astounding
exoticism of the plantings
on the Middle Terrace: a broad
band of cordylines, drooping
echiums, textural shrubs
and vibrant subtropical
flowers spreading each side
of the path.

The space between these four governing axes is divided by an informal grid of narrow cross-paths that lead to or encircle a series of individual gardens. These include the ruins of the old abbey; an artistic arrangement of palms; beds outlined with pebbles in the shape of the Union Jack; a Mediterranean garden bursting with olives, cork oaks, aloes, scented herbs and flowers; and a shrine-like enclosure dominated by David Wynne's wonderfully tactile marble statue of Gaia. Other bold contemporary sculptures – Cornishman Tom Leaper's life-size bronze agave and Lucy Dorrien-Smith's shell house in the Mediterranean garden, Wynne's joyous and *mouvementé* trio of children outlined against the sky and sea – are strong enough in scale and presence to stand up to the dominance of the natural world. Such is the luxuriance of the plantings, however, that all these things are screened and sometimes concealed by the prodigious growth of vegetation and flowers.

Tresco has had its dark days, both human and horticultural. During the Second World War all four Dorrien-Smith brothers served in the army; three of them were killed, two of them on the same day. Then, in January 1987, a ferocious fortnight of snow, ice and freezing temperatures saw swathes of the garden decay and disintegrate during the months that followed – 80 per cent of the plant population was lost, including complete collections built up over the previous century. No sooner had the devastation been repaired with brisk and unstinting assistance from individuals and botanic gardens nationwide than the hurricane that devastated the south of England hit on 25 January 1990. The reaction of Tresco's garden curator Mike Nelhams on that infamous day was initially somewhat inappropriate: he noticed that the wind was 'getting up a bit'. Having got up to 127 miles per hour, it proceeded to demolish or uproot 600 mature trees and destroy 90 per cent of the shelterbelt planted in the two decades after 1870.

Although plants grow extraordinarily quickly at Tresco, the shallow root system of many of the shelterbelt trees means that they die quickly too. The regenerative power of the microclimate is such, however, that twenty years and sixty thousand newly planted trees later, the garden is as well protected as it has ever been, with *Cupressus macrocarpa*, *Pinus radiata* and

LEFT The ruined arch of the ninth-century Benedictine priory has acquired colonies of sempervivums and agapanthus, turning it into a bizarre version of a Cornish hedge. In front is a fan palm; behind, a sheltering rampart of *Quercus ilex*.

LEFT Cordylines, *Agave salmiana* var. *ferox*, sempervivums and a range of other succulents embroider a corner of the Middle Terrace.

P. muricata the stalwarts, protectively reinforced by a range of tough ornamentals: metrosideros, eucalyptus, araucarias, nothofagus, podocarpus and agathis.

Within the encircling belt are sometimes towering and always eye-catching individuals: thirty-five species of banksia, including *B. grandis* with evergreen leaves dovetailed neatly beneath its fat sausage-flowers; 60-foot/18-metre *Metrosideros excelsa* entirely covered in July with fluffy red globes; Norfolk Island pines (*Araucaria heterophylla*) that have been known to reach 90 feet/27.5 metres. Palm trees, lower-growing but unmistakable of outline, include rhopalostylis from New Zealand, *Phoenix canariensis* and the Chilean wine palm (*Jubaea chilensis*); shorter still but equally dominant, the tree ferns *Dicksonia antarctica* and black-trunked *Cyathea medullaris*. Making as much impact as any of these are *Quercus ilex* hedges planted as free-standing screens at key points in the garden; they are kept clipped to 35 feet/10.5 metres, the maximum extension of the pruning ladders.

But it is the number and range of exotic flowers – some tumbling from climbers and tall trees but very many at eye or ground level – spread across every part of the garden that are guaranteed to take your breath away. A National Collection of acacias sprawls or climbs its way over the hillsides; agaves, yuccas and furcraeas for once fit into the show rather than running away with it; echiums, isoplexis, musschias and hedychiums flourish their mammoth pyramidal flower spikes and beschornerias and watsonias their sword-like leaves; hanging trumpet flowers like iochroma, brugmansia and correa are matched leaf for leaf and bloom for bloom by succulents, bromeliads and daisies; and those strange but now familiar strays from the animal kingdom *Strelitzia reginae* and *Clianthus puniceus* brandish their beaks and claws along the terraces.

The distinction that's often made but needs to be remembered is that although Tresco has an unrivalled botanical collection it is not a botanic garden. Plants are not required to be rigidly separated by zone or genus, and this gives Dorrien-Smith, Nelhams and head gardener Andrew Lawson freedom to distribute the 3,500-strong collection not only according to the plants' natural preferences but also to aesthetic advantage. The collection is being increased these days thanks to the networking brotherhood of botanic gardens across the world.

Boundaries continue to be pushed out all the time, as plants on the very edge of the island's climatic zone are tested. Efforts with bougainvilleas and strelitzias have not met much success so far, but the well-knit and creative team will persevere, as they will with the newest venture – the establishment of a rose collection, in which they've joined forces with Carolyn Hanbury and the gardeners of the famous Anglo-Italian garden of La Mortola and with Mattocks Roses. Bounce back, leap forward – as a motto not the greatest (sounds better in Latin when translated for me as *Resurgit exsilitque*), but it seems to sum up the spirit of Tresco.

OPPOSITE, CLOCKWISE FROM TOP LEFT On Tresco, agapanthus count as weeds; the shell house decorated by Lucy Dorrien-Smith looks over the Mediterranean garden; a corner in the upper part of the garden; the shell-encrusted interior of the Valhalla has a collection of figureheads taken from wrecked ships.

LEFT The strangely bifurcated trunk of a Monterey pine at the top of the Middle Terrace.

The Minack Theatre

In 1761 the 4th Earl of Dunmore erected a gazebo topped by a gigantic pineapple in the walled kitchen garden of his estate in Stirlingshire. A couple of decades later the Bishop of Derry and Earl of Bristol, the notorious Earl Bishop, was inspired to build himself a circular summer library modelled on the Temple of Vesta in Rome, 120 feet/36.5 metres above the sea in County Londonderry. The Minack Theatre is a present-day folly of a very Cornish kind, one virtually wrested from the sea, sculpted out of naked rock and hung with exotic flowers.

The theatre was levelled, shaped, motivated and financed in the 1920s and 1930s by a remarkable woman, Rowena Cade. Situated on the very tip of the county, further south even than Land's End, it occupies one curve of the Porthcurno Beach horseshoe, and its coordinates are a trio of rocks; the Lizard and its lighthouse close off the view on the horizon. Miss Cade took it upon herself to hew and hack at the vertical cliff face, working it into terraces buttressed by rocky blocks and bolsters punctuated by steps and paving leading down to the stage and its superb backdrop of the English Channel. Age and years of exposure to wind and spray may have wearied Miss Cade, but they never defeated her. She was physically engaged with her beloved theatre until shortly before her death at the age of eighty-nine in 1983; and an annual season of summer plays still takes place there.

An exotic little garden perched on top of the cliff introduces the bold and wildly colourful subtropical plantings she envisaged free-falling down to the sea, inserted into the rocks and along beds gouged out between them: aeoniums, aloes, *Agave attenuata*, *Carpobrotus edulis*, *Strelitzia reginae* and a sheet of ice plants, standing out among commoner garden plants like purple-flowered hebes, sea lavender, erigeron, Welsh poppies and kniphofias.

The Minack is a fabulous fireworks display, visible not only as a backdrop to the performances taking place on stage but also as an eye-catcher for mariners. It may have been created by a lady from Cheltenham, but it is a place – rocky, eccentric, free-spirited – that Cornwall is proud to claim as its own.

LEFT Lashed by the seas off the dangerous coast, lying further south even than Land's End, the Minack was created by the single-minded vision, grit and determination of a remarkable woman who harnessed the county, the *literati* and elemental nature to her cause.
RIGHT The theatre falls in terraces to the stage levelled out by hand above the rocky foreshore; the amphitheatre thus created is interspersed with exotic plants sprouting along paths and steps and from fissures in the rock.

OPPOSITE, CLOCKWISE FROM TOP LEFT Ice plants emerge from the boulders piled high at the top of the terraces; the theatre at the topmost level; a stone bench backed by a wall of ice plants; a colourful planting of exotics flanking the steps down to the amphitheatre.

RIGHT ABOVE The area leading down to the visitor centre sets an appropriately exotic tone for the terraces dropping steeply down behind the building to the sea; echiums tower among agaves, aeoniums and many other subtropical plants. RIGHT BELOW Boulders play an important role, anchoring the groups of plants into their exotic setting.

Visiting the gardens

The details given here are correct at the time of going to press, but it is always wise, before setting out to visit a garden, to telephone or consult the website.

Antony, Torpoint PL11 2QA
01752 812191, www.nationaltrust.org.uk/antony
Open end March–May, daily except Friday, Saturday and Sunday, end May–October, daily except Friday, 11.00 a.m.–4.30 p.m., last entry 4.00 p.m.

Barbara Hepworth Sculpture Garden, Barnoon Hill, St Ives TR26 1AD
01736 796226, www.tate.org.uk/stives
Open daily all year round 10.00 a.m.–5.20 p.m., last entry 5.00 p.m. (November–February closes 4.20 p.m., last entry 4.00 p.m.)

Bosvigo, Bosvigo Lane, Truro TR1 3NH
01872 275774, www.bosvigo.com
Open March–September, daily, 11.00 a.m.–6.00 p.m.

Caerhays, Gorran, St Austell PL26 6LY
01872 501310, www.caerhays.co.uk
Open mid-February–early June, daily, 10.00 a.m.–5.00 p.m., last entry 4.00 p.m.

Chygurno, Lamorna, Penzance TR19 6XH
Robert and Carol Moule, 01736 732153
Open April–September, Wednesday and Thursday, 2.00 p.m.–5.00 p.m.

Cotehele, St Dominick, Saltash PL12 6TA
01579 351346, www.nationaltrust.org.uk/cotehele
Open daily all year round, dawn–dusk

The Eden Project, Bodelva, St Austell PL24 2SG
01726 811911, www.edenproject.com
Open daily all year round except 24 and 25 December, times vary

Glendurgan, Mawnan Smith, Falmouth TR11 5JZ
01326 252202, www.nationaltrust.org.uk/glendurgan
Open mid-February–July, Tuesday–Saturday, August, Monday–Saturday, 10.30 a.m.–5.30 p.m.

Heligan, Pentewan, St Austell PL26 6EN
01276 845100, www.heligan.com
Open daily all year round except 24 and 25 December, 10.00 a.m.–6.00 p.m., last entry 4.30 p.m. (October–March closes 5.00 p.m., last entry 3.30 p.m.)

Lamorran, Upper Castle Road, St Mawes TR2 5BZ
Robert and Maria Dudley-Cooke, 01326 270800, www, lamorrangarden.co.uk
Open April–September, Wednesday and Friday, 11.00 a.m.–5.00 p.m.

Lanhydrock, Bodmin PL30 5AD
01208 265950, www.nationaltrust.org.uk/lanhydrock
Open daily all year round, 10.00 a.m.–6.00 p.m., last entry 5.30 p.m.

Marsh Villa, St Andrew's Road, Par PL24 2LU
Judith Stephens, 01726 815920, www.marshvillagardens.com
Open April–October, Sunday–Wednesday, 10.00 a.m.–6.00 p.m.

The Minack Theatre, Porthcurno, Penzance TR19 6JU
01736 810181, www.minack.com
Open daily except 25 and 26 December, 10.00a.m.–5 p.m. (November–March closes 4.00 p.m.)

Mount Edgcumbe, Cremyll, Torpoint PL10 1HZ
01752 822236, www.mountedgcumbe.gov.uk
Open April–September, 11.00 a.m.–4.30 pm, last entry 4.00 p.m. (park opens daily all year round 8.00 a.m.–dusk)

St Michael's Mount, Marazion, Penzance TR17 0EF
01736 710507, www.stmichaelsmount.co.uk
Open April–July, daily, August and September, Thursday and Friday, 10.30 a.m.–5.00 p.m., last entry 4.15 p.m.

Trebah, Mawnan Smith, Falmouth TR11 5JZ
01326 252200, www.trebah-garden.co.uk
Open daily all year round, 10.00 a.m.–5.30 p.m., last entry 4.00 p.m.

Tregrehan, Par PL24 2SJ
Tom Hudson 01726 814389, www.tregrehan.org
Open mid-March–May, Wednesday–Friday, Sunday and Bank Holiday Mondays, 10.30 a.m.–5.00 p.m.

Trelissick, Feock, Truro TR3 6QL
01872 862090, www.nationaltrust.org.uk/trelissick
Open daily all year round except 1 January, 11 a.m.–4.00 p.m. (February–October 10.30 a.m.–5.30 p.m.)

Tremenheere, Long Lane, Ludvan, Penzance TR20 8YL
Dr Neil Armstrong and Dr Jane Martin, www.tremenheere.co.uk
Open end April–October, Saturday, Sunday and Bank Holiday Mondays, 10.00 a.m.–5.00 p.m.

Trengwainton, Madron, Penzance TR20 8RZ
01736 363148, www.nationaltrust.org.uk/trengwainton
Open mid-February–October, 10.30 a.m.–5.00 p.m.

Tresco Abbey, Tresco, Isles of Scilly TR24 0QQ
01720 422849, www.tresco.co.uk
Open daily except 25 and 26 December, 10.00 a.m.–4.00 p.m.

Trevarno, Crowntown, Helston TR13 0RU
01326 574274, www. trevarno.co.uk
Open daily except 25 and 26 December, 10.30 a.m.–5.30 p.m.

Trewidden, Buryas Bridge, Penzance TR20 8TT
01736 363021, www.trewiddengarden.co.uk
Open mid-February–September, Wednesday–Sunday (July and August daily), 10.00 a.m.–5.30 p.m., last entry 4.30 p.m.

Trewithen, Grampound Road, Truro TR2 4DD
Michael and Sarah Galsworthy, 01726 883647, www.trewithengardens.co.uk
Open March–September, Monday–Saturday (plus March–May, Sunday), 10.00 a.m.–4.30 p.m.

Index

Acknowledgments

Thanks are above all to the owners and staff of all these gardens, private and public, for giving unstintingly of their time and expertise and for making every visit a positive pleasure.

To Helen and Gilbert McCabe, whose hospitality over a memorable few days kickstarted the project, and to Jeremy Nichols, whose house, centrally poised near Truro, became my base camp and refuge.

To strangers encountered in gardens, on beaches and coast paths, in pubs and cafes, whose insights into the county were often amusing and sometimes illuminating.

Finally – following the precedent set by Nikolaus Pevsner, who famously dedicated one volume of his *Buildings of England* to the ice lolly – to the glorious coffee pod, without which this book would never have been finished.